Plays by Paco Bezerra

Plays by Paco Bezerra

Cutting-Edge Spanish Theatre

Grooming
Lord Ye Loves Dragons
Lulú
I Die for I Die Not

PACO BEZERRA
Translated and edited by
ANTON PUJOL

methuen | drama
LONDON • NEW YORK • OXFORD • NEW DELHI • SYDNEY

METHUEN DRAMA
Bloomsbury Publishing Plc
50 Bedford Square, London, WC1B 3DP, UK
1385 Broadway, New York, NY 10018, USA
29 Earlsfort Terrace, Dublin 2, Ireland

BLOOMSBURY, METHUEN DRAMA and the Methuen Drama logo are trademarks of
Bloomsbury Publishing Plc

First published in Great Britain 2023

Cover design: Rebecca Heselton
Cover image © malerapaso/iStock

A catalogue record for this book is available from the British Library.

A catalog record for this book is available from the Library of Congress.

ISBN: PB: 978-1-3503-6756-2
        ePDF: 978-1-3503-6758-6
        eBook: 978-1-3503-6757-9

Series: Methuen Drama Play Collections

Typeset by RefineCatch Limited, Bungay, Suffolk
Printed and bound in Great Britain

To find out more about our authors and books visit www.bloomsbury.com
and sign up for our newsletters.

Contents

Introduction 1

Translator's Notes 7

Grooming 9

Lord Ye Loves Dragons 45

Lulú 85

I Die for I Die Not 115

Introduction

In Paco Bezerra's *From Within the Earth* (2007), Indalecio, the main character, states that 'writing is like unveiling a mystery. There are no maps that lead to hidden treasures, and there is never an X that marks the coveted ending.' I would argue that reading or watching one of Bezerra's plays supports Indalecio's claims: a mystery opens and leads you down unexpected paths to shocking revelations. The plays are always distinctive, always surprising, which may explain why, in a very short time, Bezerra (Francisco Jesús Becerra Rodríguez, Almería, 1978) has become one of Spain's pre-eminent, most celebrated playwrights. He won the Community of Madrid's Young Creators Theatre Award in 2005; Honourable Mention for the Lope de Vega Prize, 2009; the Almería Abroad Promotion Award, 2009; the award for Best Dramatic Author at the XXI GETEA International Congress in Buenos Aires, 2012; the Eurodram Award, 2014; and the Cerino Award for Best Author at the 64th International Festival of Classical Theatre in Mérida, 2018, among many others. He was also a finalist for the Caja Madrid Express Theatre Award, 2002; the Romero Esteo Award, 2004; a XI Valle-Inclán Theatre Prize at the XIX Max Theatre Awards, 2017; a XVI Premi Europa per il Teatro prize, 2017; and an ACE (Association of Entertainment Critics of Argentina) Award, 2018. His latest play, *I Die for I Die Not: The Double Life of Teresa*, included in this volume, was awarded the SGAE (Sociedad General de Autores Españoles) Prize for Best Theatre Play in 2021 and chosen as one of five plays to be performed by the European Theatre Project's Prospero Extended Network in 2022. Last year, Bezerra's complete works were published under the title *Velocidad mínima: El teatro viene después* [*Minimum Speed: Theatre Comes After*] (Ediciones la Uña Rota, 2022). His plays have been translated into twenty languages and are performed all over the world.

In Paco Bezerra's theatre, margins take centre stage, and the playwright embodies the margin. He grew up and was educated far from Madrid, without any contact that would facilitate his inclusion in a profession as inbred, to put it mildly, as the Spanish theatre. In 2017, I emailed him to ask how he had managed to integrate, and he wrote, 'I was a free bird. I did not belong to any group, nor to any mafia, nor to any particular company or theatrical family. Other playwrights or creators were part of one theatre company or another; they were assistants of such-and-such a director; they were sponsored by such-and-such theatre; but not me, always an alien.' In another interview, a reporter asked exactly where he came from, and he simply replied, 'From the street. My only recollection is that I have been walking the streets of Madrid for over twenty years.

And yes, it was very hard on me, precisely because of what you are asking me now. When I would show up anywhere, I remember everybody telling me: "But you don't look like a playwright. Are you really the one who wrote this?" My appearance or image has always detracted from my credibility.' He arrived in Madrid to study acting, but his classes in dramatic writing at RESAD (Real Escuela Superior de Arte Dramático) and the William Layton Theatre Laboratory radically changed his trajectory.

Bezerra had his own ideas about what playwriting entails. He avoids trends and preconceptions about what theatre should be. The subtitle of his complete works provides an important clue: theatre comes after. In his introduction to *Velocidad mínima*, he posits: 'a playwright writes dramatic literature; he does not write theatre', by which he means that he writes for readers, and they are free to experience the text in whatever way they desire. He hardly ever participates in the production of his plays. He says that once he has finished writing the play, his job is done, and staging his words is someone else's task. Not surprisingly, his works do not rely on the usual theatrical conventions. For example, there are no scenes: there are parts or episodes. We do not know whether certain lines in the text will be projected on an on-stage screen or only serve readers and are not part of the performance. His language is precise, alternating between the poetic and the realistic, and parallels the jarring, ambivalent conflicts he locates in strange settings: both features prevent us from drawing easy conclusions. Combined with stage directions that read like authorial observations in a novel, they present uncomfortable, multilayered truths about the human condition. Readers are always left with more questions than answers; endings are other beginnings. His plays are texts, or his texts are plays, for us to ponder.

Most of Bezerra's plays dramatize the margin, either through the characters, themes or situations. He usually presents women, immigrants, homosexuals, victims of sexual abuse and bullying, who are struggling to matter. Their marginalization, whatever its root, propels the dramatic arc, as they suffer and protest society's biases. Their plights result from their particular environments, which relentlessly try to debase them. In *Lulú* and *I Die for I Die Not*, Bezerra dramatizes two women whose stories have been silenced or heavily manipulated by the powers-that-be; two women whose agency has been stolen by their respective hegemonic narratives. Bezerra gives them voice, offering a contradictory perspective that challenges what we believe or, more important, what we have been told to believe.

He takes a similar approach in his plays based on the classical figures of Phaedra and Oedipus. Instead of writing adaptations, he investigates the meaning of these archetypes and why they still intrigue audiences. In *Phaedra's Heart*, he reclaims Euripides' original lost version. As Bezerra explains in the introduction to *Velocidad Mínima*, the first version was rejected because audiences deemed the central female character morally unacceptable. Bezerra crafts a new Phaedra, a woman who is not ashamed of her feelings. 'As soon as I saw him, I knew it would be the worst of my martyrdoms', she says about the moment she met her stepson Hippolytus, and instead of recoiling, she accepts her imminent doom. She might be burdened, but she is not ashamed.

Bezerra establishes a similar dialogue with *Oedipus*. His version moves away from the taboos of incest and patricide to humanize a character who tries to understand the fate he has been dealt. In Bezerra's universe, Oedipus' mission has nothing to do with oracular prophesy but with handling his reality the best he can. He is a victim, but not of his own doing.

In *The Little Pony*, Luismi is the composite of two boys, Grayson Bruce and Michael Morones, who suffered horrific bullying. Luismi never appears on stage; instead, his parents argue over his decision to take a Little Pony backpack to school. At the end, Bezerra dedicates the work, not only to the two persecuted boys, but 'to all the children who, like them, have suffered insults and aggressions without anyone around them doing anything to prevent it'.

This expression of outrage could well be added to almost all his works. Bezerra presents characters who cannot escape their unfair fate and whose society acquiesces to their misfortunes with glee. Nonetheless, Bezerra is too shrewd a playwright to offer dogmatic or preachy readings. Ideologically, he remains on the sidelines and leaves analysis to the audience.

The four plays included in this volume exemplify some of the themes outlined above. *Grooming* presents a cat-and-mouse game between 'Man' and 'Girl'. Although their names, Cecilio and Carolina, are revealed in the dialogue, the stage directions refer exclusively to Man and Girl. As usual in Bezerra's works, nothing is what it seems; here, he lays out a morally ambiguous scenario that the audience will have to connect like puzzle pieces but will be unable to finish. Building on the deceitful online relationship that Cecilio has established with Carolina, a lewd act on stage leads to her blackmail and the threat of endless abuse. Soon, however, the tables turn: she entraps him, proposing a quid pro quo based on an alphabet of paraphilias that she claims afflict them both.

Lord Ye Loves Dragons presents a dystopia that, written ten years ago, effectively foreshadows our present world. The depressing building where the action takes place is described as a mammoth beehive on the outskirts of a large metropolitan area. Four women inhabit different apartments in this cheap public housing, and mysterious events unfold. A mother and daughter, Chinese immigrants, live together in a basement flat, while Magdalena and Amparo live on the tenth and fifth floors, respectively. The plot revolves around a ghostly figure who roams the building wrapped in a blanket. Magdalena blames her Chinese neighbours and accuses them of housing more people than legally permitted and running an illegal operation with street vendors. Later, she blames Amparo's daughter, a substance abuser. A TV news broadcast intermittently informs the audience about the repercussions of the country's economic recession and catastrophic unemployment. To make matters worse, the city is engulfed by a rare fog, so thick that people cannot distinguish night from day. The play's title is based on an ancient Chinese proverb that means be careful what you wish for because it might come true, and the results might be devastating. If in *Grooming*, we had a cat-and-mouse game, here we encounter a beehive where a stringent hierarchy must be observed at all times.

Lulú starts out, like *Lord Ye*, shrouded in mystery. The appearance of an unconscious, injured, half-naked woman under a tree in the middle of the night frames the play in a liminal space that defies any likely conjecture. It might be a nightmare, a recollection, a fantasy, or all of them combined. The first part focuses on Amancio, an older man, who recounts several episodes of his life; mainly, the death of his wife from a snake bite near the tree where now he has encountered the unconscious woman. Amancio owns a large orchard, which is run by his two sons, Calisto and Abelardo. When the woman awakens, the three men take her into their house to heal her wounds, but apparent joy is soon followed by horror. Now Julián is introduced to parse the situation, citing specific passages from the Bible to raise questions about Adam's wives relevant to the woman's attempt to escape. The creature Amancio found, Julián argues, must be an incarnation of Adam's first wife, Lilith, who, like Adam, was created from the dust of the Earth. Refusing to submit to Adam's authority, she decided to leave Paradise, and God condemned her to wander by turning her into a night creature, history's first vampire according to some scholars, who seduces men. In other tales, she is part-woman, part-serpent, and in still others, the snake who tempted Eve. In any case, Lilith is presented negatively and must be eliminated since she perturbs the traditional narrative that puts women below men and demands their submission. Then the play diverts, not in a coup de théâtre, since Bezerra avoids flashy denouements, but as an invitation to consider the other side. Looking back, Bezerra wrote, he had established who was right and who was wrong too soon, but I disagree. Towards the end of the play, the still nameless woman the men have nicknamed Lulú says, 'Once a lie is constantly repeated, falsehoods, slowly but surely, begin to appear as the truth. The secret lies in creating a parallel explanation that hides everything we want concealed.' It is not about who is right or wrong but rather how, from a very early age, we are constantly fed narratives that we are not even interested in questioning, let alone challenging. *Lulú* might seem an easy play at first, even sentimental, but the terrain becomes muddy, and everything and everyone in it collapses.

The last play included in this volume, *I Die for I Die Not: The Double Life of Teresa*, has become a cause célèbre in Spain. After winning the prize for best play in 2021, it was selected for the Prospero Network and scheduled to open at Teatros del Canal, a public theatre managed by the Community of Madrid, when it was suddenly removed from the season without explanation. Bezerra took to social media to ask what had happened but to no avail. The cancellation turned out to be censorship by the conservative Partido Popular and the extreme-right Vox, which control the Madrid region. Almost a year later, no credible explanations have been given, and no production of *Teresa* is in the works. Theatre in Spain heavily depends on government and regional subventions, so producers cannot afford to ruffle feathers. The perceived problem with *Teresa* is the character and the enquiry into it that Bezerra dares to posit. While his reimagining of Phaedra and Oedipus bothered no one, Teresa de Jesús is one of the most powerful symbols of Catholic and ultranationalist Spain. Bezerra imagines a double scenario. First, he asks what would happen if Teresa Sánchez de Cepeda were to come back to life five hundred years after her death. How would a poor woman without papers or connections survive in Madrid today? He then examines how the work of Santa Teresa has been manipulated by the Catholic Church and all the conservative Spanish echelons. He dramatizes his Teresa as a cyborg, a terminator. In the opening scene of the monologue, she describes what happened to her body after her death. It was butchered, and all its parts were shipped around the world as 'incorrupt' 'relics'. At the beginning of the play, as she speaks, she is reattaching her body parts, which she has travelled all over the world to recover. She reconstructs herself. This cyborg Teresa allows Bezerra to trace the transformation of Teresa to Santa Teresa. The real Teresa wrote incessantly as an outspoken critic of the Church and its misogyny, cruelty and obsession with riches. Her Jewish lineage coupled with her many efforts to transform the Church, to make it more culturally tolerant and to create her own convents, brought her to the attention of the Inquisition, which she successfully tricked, thanks to her cunning use of the written word at a time when women were forbidden to read and write. Five hundred years later, she has been turned into the patron saint of domesticity, the Spanish empire and almost everything else that she detested in society. Bezerra dramatizes the deep disconnection between what Teresa expressed in her many books and letters and what she has come to symbolize.

These four plays prove how difficult it is to pigeonhole Bezerra's theatre. They seem to have been penned by different playwrights. They show his range, his ability to create different scenarios that express his concerns, his fears, what he perceives as injustices or simply his need to expose themes that require more discussion. His voice is a vector across margins, regardless of their roots; he amplifies their calls for attention. Bezerra uses language to frustrate expectations, putting his audience in a wait-and-see mode where nothing is what it seems. He builds his theatre on a cliff, where the inevitable fall is one step, one page, one scene – or one thick fog or blast of political wind – away.

Paco Bezerra's Bibliography

Plays

Ventaquemada (2003)
Dentro de la tierra/From Within the Earth (2007)
Grooming (2009)
La escuela de la desobediencia/The School of Disobedience (2011)
El señor Ye ama los dragone/Lord Ye Loves Dragons (2013)
El pequeño poni/The Little Pony (2016)
Lulú (2017)
El corazón de Fedra/Phaedra's Heart (2018)
Edipo: A través de las llamas/Oedipus (Through the Flames) (2021)
Muero porque no muero: La vida doble de Teresa/I Die for I Die Not: The Double Life of Teresa (2022)

Adaptation

Ahora empiezan las vacaciones/The Holidays Start Now (2012), adapted from August Strindberg's *The Pelican* (1907)

Translation

Las criadas/The Maids (2020), translation of Jean Genet's *Les bonnes* (1946)

Translator's Notes

Translation forces you to read the original work at a level you could never imagine possible. Every word, every verb and its tense, every adjective and adverb is carefully analysed and treated as if you were handling precious ingredients of an unstable potion. It is not a task for the faint of heart.

Translating theatre comes with an added complication: its immediacy. The text has to sound alive, natural, urgent. If it reads or sounds like a translation, the playwright's intent could be immediately lost. My only goal for these translations of Paco Bezerra's works was to pass on a reading or performance without linguistic burden. At the same time, I hope they convey my absolute respect for the originals. I saw the original Madrid staging of the first three and attended the reading of *I Die for I Die Not* in November 2022, which privileged me for the translation process. At some points, the reader may think that information is missing, especially about how the text might be presented on stage, but Bezerra does not offer any clues.

Other guidelines:

- I used standard, non-localized English throughout.
- The characters' names have not been translated.
- For Santa Teresa's poem and the title of the play *Muero porque no muero*, I used Eric W. Vogt's version,[1] included in his *Teresa of Avila: The Complete Poetry*.
- The Chinese dialogue in *Lord Ye Loves Dragons* is translated from the Spanish translation by Pilar González España as it appears in the original text.
- In *Grooming*, the reference to a low-cost Spanish supermarket chain, Día, has been translated as 'a cheap-ass supermarket'.

As I mention in the introduction, Bezerra argues that he writes texts that may later be staged or not; it is a codicil that his work does not fall under his control. Similarly, I believe these four translated plays are just stepping stones. A director and performers can build on them to adapt their own English-language version. They are translations for each reader and artist who dares to enter Bezerra's malleable world.

---

1 Vogt. Eric W., trans. and ed., *Teresa of Avila: The Complete Poetry* (University Press of the South, 2015).

Grooming

To Emmanuel Montes Becerra

Characters

Man
Girl

*A childish-looking **Girl** and a **Man** with a James Stewart face, but dressed and groomed like Cary Grant, are sitting on a park bench at dusk. The **Man** looks ahead. The **Girl** does too. Silence.*

Man   Julio combines his studies with playing amateur soccer for Real Madrid. One day the team's goalie is injured, and the coach tells Julio he will start the following Sunday. To celebrate his start as a first-string player for Real Madrid, Julio goes out and parties with his friends and his girlfriend. However, that same night, he is in a car accident and paralysed. He is taken to the hospital and has surgery and begins a long rehabilitation process. Gradually, his friends and his girlfriend stop visiting him, and he is left all alone.

*The **Man** and the **Girl** keep looking ahead.*

Man   Every time they showed it on television, I would happen to be at my grandmother's. She never allowed me to watch the ending. As soon as Julio went to the hospital, she would turn it off. She'd say it was too sad and she couldn't understand why they made movies like that. I would tell her that I knew, from the coming attractions, what happened next: Julio retires to a hotel where he starts singing and then becomes famous. But my grandmother would say no, no way, after what had happened to him, there was no way something good could happen.

Silence.

Do you see the asshole over there?

*The **Girl** does not answer.*

Man   He arrived a long time ago. He went to the other side of the pond at the exact point where he is right now, and he started feeding worms to the ducks. Do you think they eat the worms?

*The **Girl** does not answer.*

Man   I bet you anything he thinks that dressing up as a cockroach and feeding them that shit is very cool. That's the problem. People just don't get it. But there's nothing you can do. You can never reason with assholes because, among many other things, they never listen. And even if they did, it wouldn't matter. Do you know why?

*The **Girl** does not answer.*

Man   Assholes never understand anything you tell them. They think you are talking to them because you are as big an asshole as they are.

Silence.

Man   Very soon, going to the cinema will be history. The other day, I read in one of those newspapers that they give away for free: the ten things that will be history in ten years. Do you like movies? What's your favourite?

*The **Girl** does not answer.*

Man   The movie you've watched the most times. Have you seen *North by Northwest*?

*The **Girl** does not answer.*

Man   Cary Grant is being followed by a crop duster through the middle of a large field. He doesn't know why he's being followed. He looks for a place to hide. He sees a cornfield further away. He runs and ducks inside the cornfield. The plane searches for him and then starts fumigating, and Cary Grant nearly asphyxiates until a fuel truck appears, and Cary Grant darts out of the cornfield toward the road, but the truck doesn't stop and almost runs him over. The crop duster changes direction and flies towards him again but misses, loses control, flies into the fuel truck, and explodes, and everything is filled with gas, smoke and fire. When the camera frames Cary Grant again, he doesn't even have a scratch. Do you know why?

*The **Girl** does not answer.*

Man   Cary Grant is a hero. The total opposite of James Stewart, a traumatized and cowardly guy who spends his days in pyjamas looking at other people's lives through binoculars. I didn't know it either – I just found out that they say Cary Grant and James Stewart are the same person.

*The **Man** notices one of his shoelaces has come undone.*

Man   At first, it seems weird – two different guys can't be the same guy – but what's cool is that while Cary Grant represents what Hitchcock would like to be – a handsome and decisive guy – James Stewart reflected his real personality – a guy who was traumatized, shy and cowardly. The asshole with the duck is gone. Tie it.

*The **Girl** keeps looking ahead.*

Man   My shoe.

*The **Girl** stops looking ahead and turns her gaze towards the **Man**'s shoe.*

Man   Tie it.

The **Girl** *turns her gaze from the shoe and for the first time looks at the* **Man**.

Man   Tie it.

Silence.

The **Girl** *slowly gets up from the bench and kneels next to the* **Man**'s *shoe.*

Man   Hitchcock has helped me understand things that have nothing to do with movies or anything.

The **Girl** *grabs the* **Man**'s *shoelaces and starts tying them.*

Man   Actually, Hitchcock has helped me understand things to do with me.

The **Girl** *finishes tying the* **Man**'s *shoelaces.*

Man   Thank you.

The **Girl** *stands, then sits on the bench again and resumes looking ahead.*

Man   My name is Leonardo. My mother gave it to me. People think it was because of DiCaprio, but given the age and if you only think about it for three seconds, that just doesn't make much sense. It was because of da Vinci, the Italian who did everything. Do you know who da Vinci was?

The **Girl** *keeps looking ahead and does not answer.*

Man   I studied piano, architecture and fine arts. I had a band when I was young. I played the guitar and wrote lyrics. But cinema, movies, is what I like most. I have talent, y'know? I am an artist. The problem is that wasting time pisses me off, and I'd rather meet up with pretty girls who make me hard.

He takes a deck of cards from one his pockets and fans them out to the **Girl**.

Man   Pick a card.

The **Girl** *does not answer.*

Man   Choose.

The **Girl** *looks at the cards.*

Man   I'm sorry, but you have to choose one.

The **Girl** *thinks about it and chooses one that the* **Man** *immediately takes from her hand.*

Man   It's always the same deal. I ask you a question. If you get it right, you can turn around and go back the way you came, but if you get it wrong – You see, I have a little problem and would like to ask you a small favour. History, language and literature, art, sciences, cinema or sports?

The **Girl** *stands up.*

Man   Where are you going?

Girl   It's getting late.

Man   Sit back down, you're making me nervous.

Girl   You told me you wouldn't touch me.

Man   And I'm not gonna.

Girl   You are not sixteen.

Man   You just say that because you don't know me yet.

Girl   What do you want?

Man   History, language and literature, art, sciences, cinema or sports?

The **Girl** *is still standing.*

Girl   If I choose, will you let me go?

Man   I am not going to repeat it.

Girl   All right – history.

Man   I am waiting.

Girl   Huh?

Man   I told you to sit down.

Silence.

The **Girl** *looks down, sits on the bench again, and the* **Man** *reads the card.*

Man   Who was the first woman to travel in space: Adriana Sklenarikova, Svetlana Savitskaja, Valentina Tereshkova or Sally Ride? Time.

The **Girl** *seems to be thinking about it, but she does not answer.*

Man   Time.

The **Girl** *does not answer.*

Man   Try one – there's nothing to lose.

The **Girl** *does not answer.*

Man   Just say one. Maybe you'll get it right.

The **Girl** *does not answer.*

Man   Maybe you're lucky.

Girl   The fourth one.

Man   Sally Ride?

The **Man** *looks at the back of the card and checks the answer.*

Man   It wasn't an easy question. I'm sorry.

He gives the card to the **Girl***, so she can check the answer.*

Man   You know what's gonna happen now, don't ya?

The **Girl** *looks ahead again.*

Man   It will only last a moment. I'm not going to hurt you.

Silence.

Trust me . . .

Silence.

And everything will be okay.

He unzips his pants.

Silence.

The **Girl** *still looks ahead*

Man   You'll like it you'll see. Given the circumstances and the way the world is nowadays, I'd say that you are even lucky to have met me.

Silence.

Believe me, Carolina, it could have been a lot worse.

The **Girl** *stands up.*

Man   Turn around and kneel down.

The **Girl** *turns around and stands in front of the man. The* **Man** *takes out his penis, and the* **Girl** *kneels down. Slowly, the* **Girl** *moves her mouth to the* **Man**'s *penis and starts very softly to fellate him. The* **Girl** *continues fellating the* **Man** *until he ejaculates. He puts his penis back inside his pants. The* **Girl** *moves to one side and spits out a glob of saliva.*

Silence.

Man   You're not upset with me, are you?

The **Girl** *does not answer.*

Man   What are you going to do now?

The **Girl** *does not answer.*

Man   Aren't you going to answer me?

Girl   I guess I'll go home.

Man   Why? Aren't you sure?

Girl   Huh?

Man   Since you've said, 'I guess I'll go home', I don't know, maybe you're not sure. Maybe you live far away. Maybe you'll stay with a friend, I don't know. Maybe it's easier than all this. Or maybe you just don't want to talk to me.

The **Girl** *does not answer.*

Man   I've only met you recently, but you know what I'm thinking, Carolina?

The **Girl** *does not answer.*

Man   I think you don't trust me. Sit back down.

Girl   Sorry, but I have to get going.

Man   I've told you to sit back down. Didn't you hear me?

The **Girl** *doesn't do or say anything.*

Man   Sit back down.

The **Girl** *doesn't do or say anything.*

Man   If you want to do it the easy way, let's do it the easy way, but if you want problems –

Girl   Why are you doing this to me?

Man   Why am I doing what to you?

Girl   I'd like to go home now

Man   And what's the problem? Do you live far away?

Girl   More or less.

Man   And are you in a hurry?

Girl   We always have dinner around this hour.

Man   Then you really are.

Girl   What?

Man   I'm just mentioning it because, if you want, I can drop you nearby.

Girl   You don't have to bother.

Man   It's not a bother at all – on the contrary, my car is right there.

Girl   Don't worry, I'll take the bus.

Man   I'm not worried, but I'll just feel better.

Girl   I'm talking seriously.

The **Man** *stands up.*

Man   So am I.

The **Girl** *takes one step back.*

Man   I told you to sit back down.

Girl   I came here, and I did what you told me to – Now it's your turn.

Man   Do you know what you'll say when they ask where you've been?

Girl   I won't tell a soul.

Man   Right, but how will I know?

The **Girl** *does not answer.*

Man   I don't want any misunderstandings.

Girl   If you want me to get into your car, I'm sorry, I'm not going to do it.

Man   Why not?

Girl   Because that's not what we agreed on.

Man   When?

Girl   Last night.

Silence.

Girl   In our Messenger conversation.

INSTANT MESSAGING, MASS EMAIL OR GENERAL-PURPOSE SOFTWARE.

Never include your passwords or credit card numbers in an IM conversation. To best avoid viruses or worms, do not accept or open a file or link via IM unless you recognize the source.

Man   Just write the name and *who* after my 'Who's there?' part and write LOL if you think it's funny.

Knock knock.

Who's there?

The **Girl** *does not answer or write any questions.*

Man   Ray D.

Ray D who?

The **Girl** *does not answer or write any questions.*

Man   Ray D or not, here I come.

Silence.

Man   What's the matter? Don't you think it's funny?

Girl   Ray D? I don't know any Ray D. It's a stupid joke.

Man   Who's there?

Roach.

The **Girl** *does not answer or write any questions.*

Man   Roach who?

Roach you an email last week, and I'm still waiting for a response.

Silence.

Man   Who's there?

Euripides.

Euripides who?

Girl   No fucking clue.

Man   Euripides jeans, you pay for 'em.

Girl   Excuse me, but how do we know each other?

Man   I guess you want to change topics –

Girl   It's not that – it's just – I don't know who you are.

Man   We've been talking for a long time.

Girl   Where?

Man   In a chat room, I think.

Girl   Which chat room?

Man   Or via Twitter? I really don't remember.

Girl   How old are you?

Man   Sixteen.

Girl   What's your screen name?

Man   My what?

Girl   On Twitter, what's your screen name? I can't see your picture.

Man   Sorry, but sometimes I don't understand what you write.

Girl   On Twitter, what's your name?

Man   Danny Hotguy. I sent you some pics not too long ago in front of an octopus.

Girl   What octopus?

Man   In an amusement park, without a T-shirt. An octopus, don't you remember?

Girl   I still can't get your pic.

Man   This is not my computer.

Girl   Then we better talk another day.

Man   Wait.

Girl   Really, I have things to do.

Man   Just a sec.

Girl   I'm sorry, but I don't usually speak to people without pics.

Man   There's something important I'd like to tell you. I changed your password and your secret question. If you close Messenger, you won't be able to open it again. I have stolen your email account with all of your messages.

Silence.

If you don't change your secret question by default, the same question always pops up – 'name of pet'. The first time we chatted, I asked you if you liked animals. I told you I had a dog named Manolo, and you talked to me about your parakeet Jimmy Jimmy. I've been logging into your account for weeks now, and I see all of your pictures. I think I'm in love with you.

Silence.

I'm not sure what came over me, but – I have the feeling I would do anything you ask me to do.

On the screen, a pop-up box asks Carolina 16 to join a video conference with Mr Hitchcock. Accept/Reject.

Man   Accept, please.

*The **Girl** does not answer.*

Man   Or you will lose your account. Up to you.

*The **Girl** does not answer.*

Man   As you wish, but don't say I didn't warn you.

*The **Girl** accepts the invitation, and her image appears on the **Man**'s computer screen.*

Man   Adjust the webcam up.

*The **Girl** doesn't do or say anything.*

Man   The webcam – I'm not seeing you well.

*The **Girl** raises the webcam.*

Man   A little bit more.

*The **Girl** adjusts the webcam up to her face.*

Man   It's out of focus.

*The **Girl** moves her hand towards the webcam and slowly focuses it until the image is crystal clear.*

Man   What's your name?

*The **Girl** does not answer.*

Man   I want to hear your voice. Tell me your name.

Girl   Carolina.

Man   How old are you?

Girl   Sixteen.

Man   Lift your shirt.

*The **Girl** doesn't do or say anything.*

Man   Lift it up.

*The **Girl** doesn't do or say anything.*

Man   Please.

Silence.

*In the end, the **Girl** lifts her T-shirt and shows her breasts to the webcam.*

Man   Grab something.

Silence.

The TV remote.

*The **Girl** doesn't do or say anything.*

Man   Or a deodorant tube.

*The **Girl** grabs her cell phone.*

Man   Show it to me.

*The **Girl** shows her cell phone to the webcam.*

Man   Put it in.

*The **Girl** doesn't say or do anything.*

Man   In your mouth.

*The **Girl** opens her mouth and puts the phone close to it.*

Man   Suck it.

*The **Girl** doesn't say or do anything.*

Man   Suck it and look at me.

*The **Girl** disconnects the webcam, and her image disappears from the **Man**'s screen.*

Man   Why did you log off?

On the **Girl***'s screen, another video conference invitation pops up: Mr Hitchcock wishes to start a video conference with Carolina 16. Accept/ Reject. The* **Girl** *doesn't accept. The* **Man** *sends it again: Mr Hitchcock wishes to start a video conference with Carolina 16. Accept/Reject.*

Man   Accept.

The **Girl** *rejects the invitation, and the* **Man** *sends her a folder to download. On the* **Girl***'s screen, we see the folder icon.*

Man   It's a video. Download it.

The **Girl** *does not answer.*

Man   You look very good. Really. You're gonna love it.

Silence.

The **Girl** *finally accepts the folder, and it automatically downloads onto her computer. We hear a beep, and on her computer screen, a small video shows everything she did after she accepted the* **Man***'s video conference request: adjusting the webcam up, a little bit more, adjusting the focus, saying her name, her age, lifting up her shirt, showing her breasts, grabbing her cell phone and showing it to the webcam, opening her mouth and putting the cell phone close to it.*

Man   What would you do if I were to send this video to all of the contacts in your email account?

The **Girl** *does not answer.*

Man   Carolina, are you there?

The **Girl** *does not answer.*

Man   By the way, what are you doing tomorrow?

The **Girl** *does not answer.*

Man   By the way, one of your email contacts says 'Dad'. I guess Dad is your father.

Girl   Please don't do it.

Man   I know a place.

Girl   Don't send this video to anyone.

Man   On the other side of the bridge that divides the city, there's a park with a lake. It has four entrance gates. Do you know it?

The **Girl** *does not answer.*

Man   The north gate is closest to the pond. Once you enter, behind the stairs to the gardens, there are two paths. At the beginning of the one on the right, there's a statue of an angel with a bird on his head. Take that path, stay on it, and you'll have no problem reaching a small square without a fountain or sculpture, just a bench. Walk to the bench and sit down. Tomorrow evening at 7.30. You. Alone.

Silence.

I assure you that I am the one most interested in destroying this video and not sending it to anyone, so I hope you'll agree and give me no cause to do otherwise.

The **Man** *and the* **Girl** *still standing next to the bench. They look at each other in silence.*

Man   I don't want you to get the wrong idea about me.

Girl   The bus will be here any moment.

Man   Aren't you gonna let me finish?

Girl   I don't want to miss it.

Man   Can't you wait just one minute?

Girl   It's the last one.

Man   What does your father do?

Girl   The bus is about to arrive.

Man   Can we change the subject, or we are gonna be talking all the time about the damn bus?

The **Girl** *does not answer.*

Man   Maybe he doesn't have a job – he's unemployed.

The **Girl** *does not answer.*

Man   I don't know, Carolina. I offered to give you a ride, and you don't want to. I ask you where your father works, and you don't want to answer. But then you want me to trust you and let you go as if nothing has happened. Do you know what I mean?

Girl   I don't like talking about it.

Man   About what?

Girl   About my father.

Man   Why?

The **Girl** *shrugs.*

Man   Is he sick?

Girl   No.

Man   Then what's the matter with him?

Girl   I don't know. I've never met him. I don't even know if he exists.

Man   Must be tough.

Girl   Can I go now please?

Man   Not knowing who your father is, I mean. It must be tough.

The **Girl** *does not answer.*

Man   Do you live alone then? Do you have siblings?

Girl   You won't let me go, will you?

Man   If there's anything you want to tell me, anything – I really would like you to know, Carolina, that you have a friend here, and you can trust me.

The **Girl** *bursts into tears.*

Man   Carolina –

The **Girl** *keeps crying.*

Man   Carolina. Stop crying and look at me.

Girl   Please let me go.

Man   All right, but answer my questions.

Girl   I am an only child. I live with my mother.

Man   The two of you alone or with anybody else?

The **Girl** *falls to the ground.*

Man   Carolina, I asked you a question.

Girl   We live with her boyfriend.

Man   Your mother's.

Girl   Yes.

Man   And what does her boyfriend do for a living?

The **Girl***, still crying, does not answer*

Man   Well, he must have to get some money to eat, or doesn't he eat?

The **Girl** *seems to stop crying and looks at the* **Man** *from the ground.*

Man   What's the matter, Carolina?

Girl   Why are you asking me so many questions?

Man   And why don't you ever answer?

The **Girl** *does not answer.*

Man   Do you like to play it cool?

Girl   No.

Man   Then why don't you answer my questions?

Girl   Prestressed concrete.

Man   What is that?

Girl   I have no idea. Can I go now?

Man   You don't know?

Girl   No.

Man   What did you say it was?

Girl   Prestressed concrete.

Man   I mean your mother's boyfriend.

Girl   You're doing all this so I'll miss my bus, aren't you?

Man   I thought it was clear we wouldn't be talking about the bus anymore.

Girl   Marian.

Man   Huh?

Girl   You asked for my mother's boyfriend's name. His name is Marian.

Man   What kind of name is that? No man has that name.

Girl   He's a foreigner.

Man   From where?

Girl   From Romania.

Man   How tall is he?

Girl   Huh?

Man   Is he taller or shorter than me?

Girl   Huh?

Man   Do you think I'm an idiot?

The **Girl** *does not answer.*

Man   Answer me. Do you think I'm an idiot?

The **Girl** *does not answer.*

Man   Listen to me, Carolina – Last night when we were chatting, out of all your contacts, I could have chosen any other email address, but I specifically chose your father's. You don't even know if he exists, but he appears in your contact list. Kinda funny, isn't it?

The **Girl** *gets up and takes a step back.*

Girl   Don't you move.

The **Man** *looks at the tips of his shoes.*

Man   Have you seen me move?

Girl   If you take just one step –

Man   What?

Silence.

Girl   I'll scream.

Man   You see? Finally your true colours are showing.

Girl   If you touch me again, I swear I *will* scream.

Man   I like how you talk, the way you move your lips.

Girl   I've done my part.

Man   Do you know what's bad about lying?

Girl   Now it's your turn.

Man   That once you've been caught in a lie, you always have to tell the truth.

Girl   Not everybody is ready to hear the truth.

Man   Where did you learn to talk like this?

Girl   I listen and then I speak, in that order.

Man   That's not too difficult.

Girl   You'd be surprised. You need a lot of patience.

Man   By the way, I don't know about yours, but mine is starting to run out. Are you going to tell me what your father does for a living? Or are you going to keep playing hard to get?

The **Girl** *does not answer.*

Man   You seemed smarter via Messenger, but I guess it was just my impression.

Girl   He moved out a long time ago. He's a subway conductor. But I haven't seen him in a year and a half. After my mother kicked him out, he hasn't been around.

Man   And that thing about your mother dating a Romanian – is it true?

Girl   What does that matter?

Man   I'm just asking if it's true.

Girl   No, it's not true.

Man   And why did you lie to me?

Girl   I didn't lie to you.

Man   But you made it up.

Girl   I didn't make it up. either.

Man   Because you're the one who's going out with him, aren't you?

Girl   No. I don't have a boyfriend.

Man   Then who the fuck is dating the Romanian?

Girl   My father.

Silence.

Girl   Although, according to my mother, they'll soon break up because the Romanian has always been in love with his longtime girlfriend and not with my father.

Man   He's gay?

Girl   Who?

Man   Your father.

Girl   What do you think?

Man   Has he ever touched you?

Girl   Who?

Man   Your father. Or the Romanian?

Girl   What are you talking about?

Man   Have they ever touched you?

Girl   Do you touch your daughter while you're bathing her?

Silence.

Like most men, my father can be stupid and immature, but he's a gentleman.

Man   What did you just say?

Girl   That my father can be immature, but he's a gentleman.

Man   Before that – repeat what you just said.

Girl   I don't know what you're talking about.

Man   Repeat it!

*The **Man** goes around the **Girl** and stands behind her back.*

Man   You just got yourself into a lot of trouble, little girl. Sit back down on the bench.

*The **Girl** turns around and faces the **Man**.*

Girl   Whatever you're gonna tell me, I'm gonna hear it the same whether I'm sitting down or standing up.

Man   Why did you say that?

Girl   I think you'd rather not know.

Man   Are you messing with me?

Girl   Nope.

Man   What are the hell are you talking about then?

Girl   Your daughter. You asked me about her, didn't you?

Man   Huh?

Girl   It's funny, but every time I go there, something catches my eye. Customers, for example, just go in, grab a loaf of bread or a bag of lentils, and they're dying to get out. People hate shopping in cheap-ass supermarkets. That's why there's always fighting in the checkout lines. The aisles are so narrow – maybe if the products were placed better, people would stay longer, but then no one else could get into the store. That's why the cashiers and everybody who works there are so ugly – so clients will leave fast, and more people can get in.

The **Man** *smiles.*

Girl   Do you think that's funny?

The **Man** *stops smiling.*

Girl   I'm not trying to be funny. Some days, while your hands are freezing as you reposition bags of food in the freezer section, I dial your home intercom and say I'm with Social Services.

Silence.

Then I go up and your wife, always very kind, invites me for a coffee, and I accept because it's the polite thing to do, even though I shouldn't because coffee upsets my stomach and gives me diarrhoea. Then I ask her to please let me use the bathroom. But your apartment has a strange layout. At first it seems easy enough, but on the way out, I always open the wrong door. And without knowing how I got there, I'm in a room that looks like an office, with a laptop on a table. I always resist the temptation, but today, I don't really know why, but I couldn't, and I took it. Before coming to the park, I turned it on, and I saw it. First, my video. Then all the others, including the one of your daughter in the bathtub.

She sits back down on the bench.

I don't know if I've answered your question.

No response

Your wife is ugly as shit, but your daughter is beautiful and quite photogenic. It's not that she's ugly in real life, but she looks better in pictures. Do you take them yourself?

No response.

I'm talking about the pictures. Or do you call one of your friends to help you?

No response.

The thing about you liking movies, writing lyrics and playing guitar, it could be true. However, the thing about Leonardo and all that crap, that's a lie. You're not named for da Vinci or DiCaprio. Your name is Cecilio. And you work as a stockboy in a cheap-ass supermarket.

She pulls out a pack of cigarettes.

People don't lie because they want to.

She takes a cigarette out of the pack, and the park lamp lights up. Night has arrived.

You want a cigarette?

No response.

It's a light, although I think they contain more crap than the regular ones, and they say they're even more addictive.

Silence. The **Man** *slowly walks towards the bench and sits next to the* **Girl**, *on the side opposite to where he sat at the beginning. The* **Man** *looks ahead.*

Girl   You sure you don't want a cigarette?

Man   I don't smoke.

Girl   Good for you. It's bad for you.

She takes out a lighter, lights up and takes a deep drag.

Girl   I'm quitting.

She takes another deep drag. The **Man** *continues to look ahead.*

Girl   Tie it up.

No response.

Kneel down and tie it up.

The **Man** *looks at the* **Girl**.

Man   Who are you?

Girl   The shoe.

The **Man** *looks at the* **Girl***'s shoe. The* **Girl** *takes another deep drag.*

Girl   What are you waiting for?

The **Man** *looks at the* **Girl** *again.*

Man   It doesn't have shoelaces.

Girl   So what?

She smokes again

You just tie it up.

Silence.

Finally, the **Man** *gets up and kneels next to the* **Girl***'s shoe.*

Girl   Do you come to this park often?

No response.

During the day, it's pretty ugly, but at night, it has its charm. Same with you.

The **Man***, from the ground, looks up at the* **Girl** *again.*

Girl   Get up and sit back on the bench.

The **Man** *complies.*

Girl   G – R – O – O – M – I – N – G – grooming. Have you ever heard of it?

Man   Huh?

Girl   What does it sound like?

No response.

It sounds strange, doesn't it?

No response.

I'll tell you why. Spain is full of ignorant people who think Spanish is not technical enough and that some terms sound better in a language that no one understands. 'Cyber-sexual harassment against minors' would be much clearer. I don't know about you, but personally, I don't like 'grooming'. It's short and to the point but very ugly. What do you think?

No response.

What do you think about calling it grooming when cyber-sexual harassment works just fine?

No response.

You don't care?

No response.

About all these matters, I mean. Do you care at all?

No response.

Well, it kind of matters to you. By the way, how many accounts do you have?

Man   I'm sure we can come to an understanding.

Girl   How many girls have you recorded?

Man   Where is my computer?

Girl   I – C – U. Does it sound familiar?

Man   Where the hell is my computer?

Girl   I've been trying to tell you, but for whatever reason, you're not interested or you're just not paying too much attention. I – C – U – as in internet, C as in crimes, U as in unit – Internet Crimes Unit. Signal piracy, e-commerce fraud, child pornography and grooming cases. You pretend to be a minor, you choose a name, a screen name, you enter a chat, you wait for someone to contact you, and when you suspect someone, you trace their IP, and you investigate them in their house. That would be a case for the unit, for example.

She stands up.

This – is another one.

Silence.

The **Man** *looks at the* **Girl**

Girl   The agent continues playing the girl and shows up at the appointment time.

Silence.

The **Man** *keeps looking at the* **Girl**.

Girl   However, since the ICU cannot use minors as decoys, they need collaborators – girlish-looking actresses and things like that – although it would be ideal if they could carry it out themselves. You start early in the morning, you set all the devices, wire the girl, and check all the audio and video signals. When the time comes, the agents record the appointment from strategic locations. Some spaces are more difficult – closed spaces and the like – but in a place like this, there's never a problem. This park is big and full of trees.

Silence.

Slowly, the **Man** *looks around him.*

Girl   When the girl decides there's enough information, and the situation can't go further –

She walks to the edge of the pond. The **Man** *observes her.*

Girl   She gives the signal.

She takes an elastic band off her wrist and shows it to the **Man**.

Girl   It's always the same signal. The moment the girl pulls back her hair, all the agents on the stakeout rush out and surround the couple.

Silence.

Do you know what they do to him?

No response.

Once they surround him?

No response.

Do you know where they take him?

The **Man**, *very slowly, stops looking at the* **Girl**, *and does not even look ahead.*

Man   This morning, in my supervisor's office, where it's dank and reeks of milk, milk cartons break and milk spoils – the TV was on. All of a sudden, I recognized the dialogue. I grabbed a chair, I sat down and I watched it. It was *La vida sigue igual*. At the end, Julio sings. I've known this song all my life but never paid it too much attention. It goes like – whether you try or not, whether you win or lose, whether you triumph or sink to the bottom, whether you clean the floor or not, it will soon be full of shit again. That's what it says – that coincidences do not exist, and shit always floats. That might be the reason my grandmother never wanted me to watch it. The problem is that by the time you finally understand something, it's always already too late. You fully understand everything that matters at the exact moment when there's no turning back. Me – just in case, before going to bed, every time I shower, I pray for all the shit to go down the drain. I close my eyes and scrub hard with a sponge every single day. Every morning and every night, without fail, like clockwork, hoping that by the next day, all that shit is gone. Sometimes it works, and I can forget about it, but when I wake up – when I wake up – all the shit is there again, waiting for me. As if when I'm sleeping, I transform myself into a bug that secretes a poison that slowly seeps through my skin. The same way expired pineapple cans start oozing syrup. Hardly anyone talks about shit, but we all carry it within us. Many things in life change and transform, but others never do. Recently, I walked by my elementary school. I looked closely and saw that the metal gate was still full of graffiti. Every time I walked in or out, someone was reading them aloud. And there it was, in the same place, as if waiting for me: 'What's really unbearable in life is that nothing's unbearable.' Back then, I never understood what it meant, but now I can't agree more. Everything can be endured, anything. That's what is truly unbearable: that you can live with everything. Even with the worst thing imaginable. As horrible as it may seem.

He wakes up from his stupor and looks at the **Girl** *again. She is still by the edge of the pond holding the elastic band.*

Man   Pull your hair back.

Girl   Do you really think that a girl my age would behave the way I am in a situation like this?

The **Man** *looks at the* **Girl** *again.*

Man   The hair.

The **Girl** *does not do or say anything.*

Man   What are you waiting for?

Silence.

Pull your hair back!

He looks around again.

Man   Come on, pull your hair back!

Girl   You seemed smarter via Messenger, but I guess I was just wrong.

Man   Show it to me.

Girl   What?

Man   The badge.

Girl   What badge?

Man   Cops always carry a badge.

Girl   Not always. Only when we're on duty.

Man   And today you're on holiday?

Girl   Not exactly. It's my day off.

Man   What a coincidence.

Girl   I wouldn't call it a coincidence.

Man   What would you call it?

Girl   I think you've got me all wrong.

Man   I'm sure you make good money. I'm sure blowing strangers earns you extra pay. Come on, tell me, who the hell are you?

Girl   Cecilio, sometimes I come here alone.

Silence.

Without telling anybody.

*She puts her hand in the **Man**'s pocket.*

Man   Huh?

Girl   Let's see if you understand. I have two jobs, very different jobs, like James Stewart and Cary Grant. But, deep down, they're both the same. In one, I do what I have to do, and in the other, I do what I really like.

Silence.

You still don't realize it, but today is your lucky day. And, honestly, I'm shocked you haven't yet thanked me. I'm not sure if you're aware that, in prison, the only criminals that they isolate are terrorists and people like you.

*The **Man** looks around again.*

Girl   Who are you looking for? I told you I came alone.

*The **Man** looks at the **Girl** again.*

Girl   You don't believe me?

*She puts her hand in the **Man**'s pants and takes out the cards. She shuffles them and shows them to him.*

Girl   Choose one.

Man   Huh?

Girl   Whichever you want.

Man   Huh?

Girl   It's always the same deal. I ask you a question. If you get it right, you can turn around and go back the way you came. But, if you get it wrong – The thing is that I have a little problem myself, and I would like to ask you a small favour.

Man   Carolina –

Girl   Don't call me Carolina.

Man   What do you want me to call you?

Girl   What would you like to call me?

Man   Let's cut the crap.

Girl   Nothing would make me happier.

Man   You wanted to ask me something, didn't you?

Girl   Yes.

Man   Why don't we just do it, and stop all these questions and answers?

Girl   Because I don't like to play with an advantage.

The **Man** *gets up from the bench and starts walking towards the pond.*

Girl   Where are you going?

Man   This is crazy.

The **Girl** *gets up and goes after him. She follows him with the cards in her hand. The* **Man** *turns and stares at her. She faces him with the cards.*

Girl   I'm sorry, but in life, you have to choose.

Man   What if I don't?

The **Girl** *does not answer him.*

Man   Huh? What if I don't choose one?

Girl   I have no idea – use your imagination.

Man   What if I have no imagination?

Girl   Give it a whirl, and let's see what happens.

Long silence. The **Man** *keeps staring at the* **Girl**. *Finally, he chooses a card and hands it to her.*

Man   Happy now?

Girl   History, language and literature, art, sciences, cinema or sports?

The **Man** *thinks about it.*

Girl   Say anything. Who knows? Maybe you'll get lucky. Give it a try – there's nothing to lose.

Man   Cinema.

The **Girl** *reads the card.*

Girl   In film, how is a werewolf usually killed? Calling out its name three times, shooting it with a silver bullet, tearing its head off or taking its heart out. Time.

Silence.

Time's up.

Man   Taking its heart out.

The **Girl** *checks the answer.*

Girl   It wasn't an easy question.

She takes an envelope out her pocket and hands it to the **Man**.

Girl   I am sorry.

Man   What is this?

Girl   Read it carefully, and let me know what you think. Take your time.

The **Man** *takes the envelope, opens it and removes a sheet of paper. He unfolds it and reads:*

Man   When persistent sexual interest is no longer found in genital stimulation or accepted behaviour, it can develop into a paraphilic disorder. Smelling flowers, for instance, or seeing someone smoke, eating faeces, caressing strangers' genitals . . . According to both the World Health Organization's International Classification of Diseases and the American Psychiatric Association's DSM-IV, there are more than one hundred and thirty categorized paraphilias. According to modern medicine, there is no cure, but relapses can be prevented after treatment with medroxyprogesterone acetate. Did you know that the Monster from Amstetten, the Austrian who locked up and raped his daughter and grandchildren for years in the basement of his house, still receives hundreds of letters every day from women proposing sexual favours?

The **Man** *finishes reading and looks up and then back at the* **Girl**.

Girl   You had no idea that both you and I suffer from paraphilic disorders?

The **Man** *reads the letter silently again.*

Man   It is not true.

*The **Girl** does not answer.*

Man   This is all bullshit.

Girl   I'm afraid not, Cecilio.

*The **Man** folds the letter, puts it back in the envelope and puts the envelope on the bench.*

Girl   What are you doing?

Man   You'll have to excuse me, but this is way too much.

*The **Girl** walks to the bench and picks up the letter.*

Man   No one in their right mind would ever willingly be a part of something like this.

Girl   I believe you mean unless they were in your situation –

Man   Listen, why don't you go find someone else?

Girl   Because we're a team now.

Man   A team?

Girl   Yes, a team.

Man   Stop messing with me.

Girl   I'm not messing with you at all. The problem is you haven't realized that, given our respective situations, the only thing left for us to do is what teams do.

Man   And what do teams do?

Girl   They stay together, and they trust each other.

Man   You're fucking nuts.

Girl   Is that what you think?

Man   Yes, I think so. Of course I think so. I think so. I absolutely think so.

Girl   And can you tell me why?

Man   Because what you're proposing doesn't make any sense.

Girl   Recording naked minor girls via webcam in order to then blackmail them into giving you a blowjob in this park doesn't make much sense either.

Man   There's no comparison.

Girl   You're the one who compares, not me. And you're the one who's all judgemental.

Man   I'm not judging.

Girl   Yes you are, Cecilio. Of course you're judging. Look at me – I come here, I try to understand you, and on top of that, I explain what's wrong with you. But now that it's your turn, now that you have to make the effort to understand me, you just tell me I'm fucking nuts and full of shit. What you're saying really makes no sense. Your shit makes sense, but mine doesn't? For fuck's sake, Cecilio, I understand what's up with you – please try to understand me.

The **Man** *stares into the* **Girl***'s eyes.*

Man   Look, listen to me. I need to go. My family is waiting.

Girl   So what? You've never called to let them know you'd be late?

The **Man** *does not answer.*

Girl   This is how you thank me? Try, at least. Or are you a coward? Maybe you know that you are a coward and have trouble accepting it.

Man   I have the feeling you have the wrong guy.

Girl   Well, I think you're wrong. I think I have the perfect guy for this.

Man   Look, listen –

Girl   Everything you need is right there, inside that container.

Man   I'm sorry. I've never done anything like this.

Girl   Don't worry – there's a first time for everything.

Man   I know, but how much time?

The **Girl** *does not answer.*

Man   Have you thought about it? What about the time?

Girl   You decide how much time.

Man   I have no idea. How can I decide?

Girl   That's the kicker!

Man   You have no idea what you are talking about.

Girl   Yes, I do. As soon as we break the light bulb, you grab what's in the container, and we start.

Man   The light bulb in the lamp?

Girl   Yes, it works better if it's dark.

Man   Okay, but how deep? What's the appropriate depth?

Girl   A girl who isn't doing or saying anything is sitting on a bench in a park. Suddenly, a very well-dressed rabbit appears. The girl, for reasons we don't know, takes a liking to the animal. She decides to follow him and enters his burrow. What's the title of the movie?

Man   What are you talking about now?

Girl   You asked me my favourite movie earlier, when I sat down.

Man   Huh?

Girl   *Alice in Wonderland.* I don't know that it's my favourite movie, but it's the one I've seen the most times. I still had to answer you.

*The **Man** does not know what to say.*

Girl   I'm just telling you, so you can see that I too have learned things from movies. Things that don't have anything to do with movies or anything but things about myself.

Man   Let me ask you something. What if you can't get out?

*The **Girl** does not answer.*

Man   What if I get here late? Aren't you afraid?

*The **Girl** does not answer.*

Man   What if I abandon you? If I leave?

Girl   Just follow the instructions, and everything will be fine.

Man   I understand, but what if something goes wrong?

*The **Girl** does not answer.*

Man   What if, for whatever reason, things don't go according to plan?

Girl   Something can always go wrong whether you're walking downstairs or frying an egg.

*The **Man**, nervously, starts to unbutton the top of his shirt.*

Girl   Do you know how it ends?

*The **Man** stops unbuttoning and looks at the **Girl**.*

Girl   *Alice in Wonderland*, my favourite movie.

*The **Man** does not answer.*

Girl   Once they're inside, the burrow, the rabbit hole, transforms into something totally different. The tunnel changes directions, and both the girl and the rabbit fall into what seems like a bottomless pit.

*The **Girl**, ready to hit the lamp with the rock, moves her arm backwards to gain strength, but the **Man** holds her arm, stops her and stares into her eyes.*

Man   Why are you doing this to me? Tell me the truth.

Girl   Because last night you told me that you were in love with me. And you also said you'd do anything for me.

Silence.

Here comes the hard part. You have to show me that you really do.

*The **Man** lets go of the **Girl**'s arm. She throws the rock and shatters the lamp. Everything turns dark.*

Ablutophilia: sexual arousal is derived from the idea of or visiting shower rooms, public restrooms, saunas or public baths.

Autassassinophilia: sexual arousal derived from the idea or act of going to dangerous places or doing dangerous things.

Balloon fetish: sexual arousal is derived from watching somebody inflate, pull or pop balloons.

Cannibalism: sexual arousal is derived from the idea or act of eating or being eaten alive by your partner.

Douching: sexual arousal is derived from rinsing out the vagina with liquids.

Ecdemolagnia: sexual arousal is derived from being away from home.

Eproctophilia: sexual arousal is derived from flatulent smells.

Gomphipothic: sexual arousal is derived from the sight of the beloved's teeth.

Hybristophilia: sexual arousal is derived from the idea of, or actually having, sexual intercourse with criminals.

Iatronudia: sexual arousal is derived from getting naked in front of a doctor while faking illness.

Ipsofilia: sexual arousal is derived by the idea or act of having sexual intercourse with oneself.

Jactitation: sexual arousal is derived from boasting about one's sexual prowess.

Keraunophilia: sexual arousal is derived from thunderstorms.

Masochism: sexual arousal is derived from humiliating a sexual partner, whether physically or verbally.

Nosophilia: sexual arousal is derived from having sexual intercourse with a partner who is terminally ill.

Odophilia: sexual arousal is derived from travelling on buses, trains or any form of public transportation.

Pederasty: sexual arousal is derived from having sexual intercourse with a minor.

Somnophilia: sexual arousal is derived from caressing or performing oral sex on a sleeping person.

Taphophilia: sexual arousal is derived from being buried alive.

Urophilia: sexual arousal is derived from touching or smelling urine.

Voyeurism: sexual arousal is derived from spying on naked bodies from a hidden position.

Xenophilia: sexual arousal is derived from the presence of foreigners.

Zoophilia: sexual arousal derived only by the idea or act of sexual intercourse with one or many animals.

Dawn – a new day in the park. The **Girl** *is sitting on a mound of soil next to a shovel.*

Girl   At the end of the hole, the girl crashes to the floor –

She gets up.

She gets up and stands up straight.

She looks down and checks her body.

She checks herself to see if she's hurt and realizes she's still in one piece.

She looks around the park.

Then she starts looking for the rabbit, but it's nowhere to be found.

Silence.

It is gone.

*The **Girl**, next to the shovel, starts walking until she disappears. The stage is empty.*

Lord Ye Loves Dragons

A Mateo Linder Bettschen

Characters

Magdalena
Ms Wang
Xiaomei
Amparo

Lord Ye Loves Dragons
(popular Chinese proverb)

Time

Year 4711 of the lunisolar calendar

Place

Interior of a massive brick and concrete structure shaped like an urban hive. It towers next to the highway that both encircles and delimits the city. Residents are organized like bees in a hive: workers toil at the bottom, drones in the middle, and at the top, the queen. Each of several blocks has its own entrance.

Structure

Hell/Purgatory/Paradise

Corresponding translations of dialogue written in Mandarin are footnoted. Pinyin romanization is included to assure correct pronunciation.

Pilar González España, a sinologist, translated the original texts into Chinese along with the romanization.

Hell

A basement in the beehive building. A single bulb per corridor dimly lights the distressing and gloomy maze of storage rooms through which **Magdalena** *stumbles like an insect trapped in a glass. She is coiffed like one of those queens engraved on a coin. Distraught, she stops before a chipped door. She looks for a doorbell but can't find one, so she knocks and waits, but no one answers. She knocks again, and, suddenly, it opens by itself; no one, only darkness. Then a light goes on, and* **Ms Wang** *appears under it. She is a woman of Asian origin, wearing a shabby woollen cardigan and flip-flops with pink socks.*

Magdalena   Hello, good morning, my name's Magdalena. I live on the tenth floor. I would like a word with your daughter, if at all possible.

Ms Wang *does not move or say anything.*

Magdalena   I don't know if you understand what I'm saying. You know who I am, right?

Ms Wang (*screams*)   小妹，有个邻居敲门，现在她 在这儿，过来，快 点儿 / xiǎo mèi, yǒu gè línjū qiāomén, xiànzài tā zài zhèr, guò lái, kuài diǎn ér.[1]

Xiaomei *appears and stands next to her mother. She is barefoot and wears an oversized shirt down to her knees.*

Magdalena   Hi, good morning. I was trying to talk to your mother, but I think she hasn't understood a thing.

Silence.

I live upstairs, on the tenth floor.

Xiaomei (*in perfect English*)   My mother does not speak your language. However, I can help you if you want to tell her something.

Magdalena   Oh, Merry Christmas, by the way.

Xiaomei *does not move or say anything.* **Magdalena**, *a little dizzy, pulls her hair back.*

Magdalena   I apologize for bothering you so early, but last night – as I returned to the building from a church concert, carolers and such – but there was a group of people demonstrating in the square and the street

---

1 Xiaomei, a woman has knocked, and she is here. Come, run!

was blocked, and by the time I got to the church, it was already packed. Anyway, I decided to come back home. I'm not sure what's going on lately, but there are demonstrations all the time.

She touches her forehead again.

What I'm trying to say is that last night, as I walked in, I thought I saw something in the main hallway. And not for the first time.

Xiaomei   I'm not sure I follow. What do you mean exactly?

Magdalena   Someone in the shadows who flees the moment I enter the hallway.

Xiaomei (*pushing the door shut*)   If you don't mind, I'd rather not talk about it.

Magdalena *puts her hand on the door to stop* **Xiaomei** *from closing it.*

Magdalena   By the time I could switch the light on, there wasn't anybody there.

Xiaomei   I'm sorry, but my mother and I haven't even had breakfast yet, and we have lots to do.

Magdalena   I could hardly see anything last night, but you were coming up the stairs, so you definitely crossed paths.

Xiaomei *is still holding the door.*

Magdalena   The first time it happened, I hurried home, but last night – I'm not sure why – I chased after whoever it was. Once I got down here, there wasn't anybody – they'd vanished into thin air.

Xiaomei   I will repeat – we have things to do.

Magdalena   Will you let me finish, please?

Xiaomei   Please, I'm just telling you –

Magdalena   Enough! Answer me! What do you think happened?

Xiaomei *says nothing.*

Magdalena   That when I got down here, there wasn't a soul.

Xiaomei   What do you want me to tell you?

Magdalena   The only apartment in the basement is yours, so you have to know something.

Xiaomei   It is not the only one. There are storage rooms also.

Magdalena   I know, but storage rooms are not apartments. And only tenants have keys.

Xiaomei   Why don't you ask *all* the tenants then?

Magdalena   That's exactly what I have been doing. Why do you think I'm down here? Sorry, but you have only two options. You cooperate, or I'll report you to the police.

Xiaomei   What?

Magdalena   You heard me.

Xiaomei   Can you please tell me – what the hell have we done to be reported to the police?

Magdalena   You sell beer illegally, and you house indigents.

Xiaomei   That is not true. We do not sell anything illegally, and we do not house indigents.

Magdalena   What about that swarm of Chinese people with backpacks that goes up and down starting at midnight?

Xiaomei   As far as I know, going up and down the stairs is not a misdemeanour.

Magdalena   I know, but what they do with what's inside the backpacks sure is.

Xiaomei   As if you knew what's inside the backpacks!

Magdalena   That's for the police to find out – that's their job. This is not a hostel or a supermarket. And besides, some seniors and young kids are already scared. We've had it!

Ms Wang, *worried, looks at* **Xiaomei**.

Ms Wang (*to* **Xiaomei**)   出什么事了，小妹，有 什么问题? / Chū shénme shì le, xiǎo mèi, yǒu shénme wèntí?[2]

Xiaomei (*to* **Ms Wang**.)   没有， 没什么，是我们 的楼邻居的主席 / Méiyǒu, méi shénme, shì wǒmen de lóu línjū de zhǔxí.[3]

Ms Wang (*to* **Xiaomei**.)   那你们聊， 什么聊了这 么久? / Nà nǐmen liáo, shénme le zhème jiǔ?[4]

---

2 Is something wrong, Xiaomei? What seems to be the problem?
3 Nothing, nothing's the matter. She's the tenants' representative.
4 Why are you talking for so long?

Magdalena *starts to feel uncomfortable with the conversation.*

Magdalena   Excuse me, but you should know that it is extremely rude to speak a foreign language in front of someone who does not!

Xiaomei (*to* **Ms Wang**)   她看起来不太好 / Tā kàn qǐlái bú tài hǎo.[5]

Ms Wang (*to* **Xiaomei**)   为什么？她怎么了？/ Wèishénme? tā zěnmele?[6]

Magdalena   What?

Xiaomei (*to* **Ms Wang**)   我想她是头疼。她没 有阿司匹林了. 现在又是节日，所有店都关 了，也许她下来是为了跟我们要一片. / Wǒ xiǎng tā shì tóu téng. Tā méiyǒu āsīpǐlín le, xiànzài yòu shì jiérì, suǒyǒu diàn dōu guān le, yěxǔ tā xiàlái shì wèile gēn wǒmen yào yī piàn.[7]

Suddenly, **Ms Wang** *switches from talking to her daughter to address* **Magdalena**.

Ms Wang (*to* **Magdalena**)   您想要一片阿司匹? / Nín xiǎngyào yī piàn āsīpǐlín?[8]

Magdalena   What is she saying?

Ms Wang (*to* **Magdalena**)   还是想要虎标万金油？/ Háishi xiǎngyào hǔ biāo wànjīnyóu?[9]

Magdalena (*to* **Xiaomei**)   Is she talking to me?

Ms Wang (*to* **Magdalena**)   我肯定她用虎标万 金油就好了一点儿。我这就给她拿来。/ Wǒ kěndìng tā yòng hǔ biāo wànjīnyóu jiù hǎo le yīdiǎnr. wǒ zhè jiù gěi tā ná lái.[10]

Ms Wang *goes back inside the apartment.*

Magdalena   Where is she going now? What the heck is she doing?

Xiaomei   You haven't knocked on our door in eighteen years. Truth be told, I thought that you were here to invite my mother to lunch.

---

5 I fear she is not okay.
6 Why, what is the matter with her?
7 I think she has a migraine. She might have run out of aspirins. And since today is a holiday, everything is closed, and maybe she has come down to ask us for one.
8 Does she want an aspirin?
9 Or would she rather use Tiger Balm?
10 Tiger Balm will help her. Let me bring it right away.

Magdalena   What?

Xiaomei   That you were here to invite my mother to lunch.

Magdalena   Why would you ever think that? Why would I do such a thing?

Xiaomei   Today happens to be her birthday. That's why.

Magdalena   No, today is not my birthday. Where did you get that from? You're wrong.

Xiaomei   *My mother's* birthday, not yours!

Magdalena   Huh?

Xiaomei   I thought you were here to congratulate her.

Silence.

A coffee and some cake. This afternoon, in your apartment, at five p.m. And then I will tell you everything I know.

Magdalena   Speak clearly. Everything you know about what exactly.

Xiaomei   About the person you asked about.

Magdalena   Are you blackmailing me?

Xiaomei   Not at all. I'm doing you a favour.

Magdalena   A favour? You?

Xiaomei   Absolutely. The person you're asking about lives in the building, definitely not homeless.

Magdalena   Huh?

Xiaomei   Why do you think someone would wrap up in a blanket and cover their face with a bag?

Magdalena *does not answer.*

Xiaomei   So no one can identify them.

Magdalena   What the hell are you talking about?

Xiaomei   Didn't you just ask for my help?

Magdalena   Huh?

Xiaomei   That is all I am doing.

Magdalena   I wasn't born yesterday – you see that, don't you?

Xiaomei   Yes.

Magdalena   Yes, what?

Xiaomei *does not answer*

Magdalena   You're just saying this to confuse me, right? You're talking nonsense just to sidetrack me.

Xiaomei   Nope. I am saying it because my mother is about to die.

Silence.

Maybe not until next year if we're lucky. Not too long ago, her doctor said she had only a couple of months left.

Magdalena   Really?

Xiaomei   She suffers from intracranial atherosclerosis – hardening of the arteries in the brain. But she doesn't know it. Well, that's not true – she knows, but sometimes she forgets. It's sad, but soon she won't remember anything.

Magdalena   It's just the first week of January! Next year is twelve months away! I'm just saying it because, with all the hassle, you could have mixed it up.

Xiaomei   No, I have not mixed it up. From the hallway on up, it might be January, but from the hallway down, it is the year 4711, and the New Year is three months away. Our apartments might seem just a few floors away, but in reality, we are over two thousand years away. Maybe that's why it took you so long to come and see us.

Ms Wang *reappears. She stands next to* **Xiaomei** *and offers a little jar to* **Magdalena**. **Magdalena** *looks at the jar but does not take it.*

Ms Wang (*to* **Magdalena**)   当我弄得时候，你脸 朝上放松的躺下，为着太阳穴转圈按摩。一会儿就没事儿了。/ dāng wǒ nòng de shíhòu nǐ liǎn cháo shàng fàngsōng de tǎng xià, wèi zhe tàiyángxué zhuǎn quān ànmó. yīhuìr jiù méi shìr le[11]. (*To* **Xiaomei**.) 如果没好， 明天让她下来我给她按 摩。告诉她。 / rúguǒ méi hǎo, míngtiān ràng tā xiàlái wǒ gěi tā ànmó, gàosu tā.[12]

Xiaomei   It's a balm, Tiger Balm, for muscle aches, coughs and mosquito bites. There are two kinds, red and green. I think she thought

---

11 When she applies it, she needs to be lying down, face up, and just rub it on her temples. She will feel better right away.

12 If she does not feel better, tell her to come down, and I will massage her. Tell her.

you did not look well. She assumed you had come down because you had a headache. Or you could take it as a welcome gift for having finally deigned to visit us after so many years.

Ms Wang is still offering the Tiger Balm jar to **Magdalena**, who finally takes it. **Xiaomei** once again tries to close the door, but again **Magdalena** prevents it.

Magdalena   What about somewhere else?

Xiaomei   What do you mean?

Magdalena   The birthday party. Can it be somewhere else, or does it have to be at my place?

Xiaomei   Up to you. We will be here all day.

Magdalena   Can another neighbour join me, or do I have to host it by myself?

Xiaomei   Are you okay? Is there any problem?

Magdalena   No, I just don't know if I'm allowed to call anyone else.

Xiaomei does not answer.

Magdalena   Amparo, from the fifth floor, for example.

Xiaomei   The more I hear you talk and – do you know who you remind me of?

Magdalena does not answer.

Xiaomei   Lord Ye! Do you know who he is?

Magdalena   No, I don't believe so.

Xiaomei   A man who loved dragons. He loved them so much that they were drawn all over his house: on the sheets, walls, curtains, his pyjamas – even his whole body was tattooed with fire-breathing dragons.

Magdalena   Do you think now's the time to talk about dragons?

Xiaomei   No, it's not a story about dragons. It's a story about you.

Magdalena   Stop beating around the bush, young woman, and answer my question! Can Amparo join me? Yes or no?

Xiaomei   I'm not beating around the bush. I'm only warning you. But it's fine with me if you'd rather not hear the story.

Magdalena   Do I invite her or not?

Xiaomei   As you wish. I am only asking for a coffee and a piece of cake. That's it. This afternoon, at five, in your apartment.

Magdalena   Fine.

Xiaomei   Perfect.

Magdalena   Five, you said?

Xiaomei   Yes, at five p.m.

Magdalena   All right.

Xiaomei   We will be very punctual.

The hall light flickers. When **Magdalena** *turns to see what's going on,* **Xiaomei** *closes the apartment door. Now* **Magdalena** *is completely alone. A haunting, telluric sound – a mixture of chimes, wind and fire – rumbles far away but approaches, like a cloud of millions of bumblebees. Once this buzzing stops, a cadenced, electric military march starts.* **Magdalena** *covers her ears. The light bulb shatters in a thousand pieces, and everything goes pitch black.*

Purgatory

Fifth floor. **Amparo**'s *living room. She is younger than* **Magdalena**, *a bit overweight, wearing a colourful sweater. The prominently displayed Christmas tree is drenched in tinsel, and the copious lights, intense as insects' eyes, blink all the time. The apartment is small, messy and tacky.* **Amparo** *is sitting in front of the stupid* **TV News** *programme with a blanket over her legs. She eats turrón while doing a crossword puzzle.*

TV News   This morning, the prime minister met with top representatives from the seventeen provinces. They all agreed to the deficit reduction goals set for the coming years. The economy is still in recession, and unemployment is at an all-time high. The prime minister announced that a financial bailout is imminent.

The doorbell rings. **Amparo** *grabs the remote and lowers the TV volume a bit.*

Amparo   Who's there?

TV News   The government just announced that the national outlook is critical and challenging –

The doorbell rings again.

Amparo   Who's there?

TV News   – because the number of citizens registered for unemployment benefits –

Amparo *kicks off the blanket, gets up, puts her crossword puzzle magazine on the table and walks towards the door, still holding a piece of turrón. The doorbell rings again.*

Amparo   Coming, coming!

TV News   – rose by three hundred thousand during the year that just ended.

Amparo *peers through the peephole and opens the door. It is* **Magdalena.** *The* **TV News** *is still on.*

Magdalena   May I come in?

Amparo   You could take it easy with the doorbell.

Magdalena   Come on, let me in.

Amparo   What's with the sour face? Where are you coming from this early?

Magdalena *walks into the living room.*

Magdalena   I couldn't sleep a wink last night. I was about to call you, but it was too late, and I didn't want to bother you.

TV News   As a result, today – now that the last quarter numbers are in –

Amparo *closes the door and walks back into the living room.*

– unemployment is at a record high –

Magdalena   And you, what are you doing?

Amparo   Same old, same old. Crosswords and getting fat. The only difference between me and a pig is that I can hold a conversation and, sometimes, I even finish a crossword.

TV News   – reaching, for the first time in history, six million two hundred thousand unemployed people.

Magdalena   You're exaggerating.

Amparo   Exaggerating? I had breakfast half an hour ago, and I'm already eating my first piece of turrón. You think that's normal?

Magdalena   Lately, nothing seems normal, so you better not ask me what normal is – I'd probably be wrong.

Amparo   Well, I can't tell you if it's the cold weather, Christmas or what the heck is wrong with me, but I feel like we're in the middle of a war. I am starving. And you still haven't said what's wrong with you.

She turns like a top to display her outfit.

Didn't you notice it?

TV News   Last year, five hundred families were evicted, while over the last five years, approximately half a million have lost their homes.

Amparo   Isn't it cute? I bought it during the Christmas sales.

TV News   Reports of violence and daylight muggings are increasing throughout the country. The police are failing to restore order.

Magdalena   The sweater?

TV News   Spending on health services and public education is being slashed, directly impacting thousands of workers –

Amparo   What's the matter? You don't like it?

Magdalena   Yes, yes, I like it – it's very pretty. I love it.

Amparo   Two for the price of one. Same sweater but different *estampado*. What do you think?

Oh, I didn't offer you turrón. Do you want some?

Amparo *offers* **Magdalena** *a piece of turrón.*

Magdalena   No, thanks. Can't eat anything. My stomach is *un puño.*

Amparo   It is hard as a rock, but if you put it near the heat, it softens quickly.

Magdalena   Really, I'm not hungry. Thank you very much.

Amparo (*biting the turrón*)   I prefer my turrón hard.

TV News   Small bank closures, strikes at the main airports, abandoned train stations, shortage of hospital staff and many other problems only confirm that demonstrations will be more frequent and larger.

Magdalena   Could you lower the volume, please?

Amparo   The TV?

Magdalena   Yes, I'd like to tell you something.

TV News   Although minimum services are not being met, and garbage piles on the street because it is not being picked up, politicians don't feel responsible.

Amparo   Can't you tell me like this?

TV News   Demonstrations . . .

Magdalena *grabs the remote and turns off the TV.*

Amparo   Magdalena, girl, don't scare me.

Magdalena   Last night I saw that thing again.

Amparo   What?

Magdalena   In the hallway.

Intrigued, **Amparo** *puts her piece of turrón on her lips and starts nibbling at it as if she were a squirrel while closely observing* **Magdalena**.

Magdalena   You'll think I've gone mad, but instead of taking the elevator, I ran after it.

Amparo *stops nibbling and puts her hands down.*

Amparo   After the homeless guy with the blanket?

Magdalena   Yes, all the way to the basement, but no one was there by the time I got there.

Amparo   What do you mean no one was there?

Magdalena   It had disappeared.

Amparo *looks at* **Magdalena**, *incredulous yet fearful.*

Magdalena   How do you think I'm doing?

Amparo   What do you mean?

Magdalena   In general, honestly. You know me well.

Amparo   Why are you asking me this?

Magdalena   I went back down there this morning.

Amparo   You did what?

Magdalena   Actually, that's where I'm coming from.

Amparo   From the basement?

Magdalena   Yes.

Amparo   What did you go down there for?

Magdalena   I went to the Chinese women's apartment.

Amparo   Which Chinese women?

Magdalena   The ones who live in the basement. Which other Chinese women would I be talking about?

Amparo   You?

Magdalena   Yes.

Amparo   Why would you do such a thing?

Magdalena   Well, I don't know. I went down there, and I knocked on their door.

Amparo   You're kidding, right?

Magdalena   No, I am not.

Amparo   How on earth could you go down there, with those two weirdos? How could you? Every time you see them on the street, you have to look away and spit because you say they give you hives.

Magdalena *takes a little jar out of her pocket and gives it to* **Amparo**.

Magdalena   Headaches, cough and mosquito bites. Tiger Balm comes in two colours: red and green.

Amparo *takes the jar from* **Magdalena** *'s hand.*

Magdalena   They just gave it to me.

Amparo *examines the jar and looks at her neighbour again.*

Amparo   I can't believe you.

Magdalena   According to the girl, it is not someone from the street – the homeless with the blanket. And it has nothing to do with them. It's someone who lives in the building, a neighbour. That's why it's always covered with a blanket.

Amparo   I hope you're kidding, but it's no longer funny.

Magdalena   I'm not kidding.

Amparo   Well, then, change your tone because you're scaring me.

Magdalena   You might not believe what I'm about to say, but – I just invited them for coffee.

Amparo   Who did you invite?

Magdalena   It was the girl's condition. If I wanted to know which neighbour it was, I had to invite her mother for coffee. Coffee and a piece of cake. This evening, at my place, five p.m.

Amparo   You're joking!

Magdalena   It's her birthday, apparently.

Amparo   Whose birthday?

Magdalena   The mother's.

Amparo   Listen, Magdalena. I'm not sure what this is all about, but there is something called the police. You call them, tell them what's going on; they come, and they solve your problem. You do *not* have to take care of everything that takes place in the building, even if you are the tenants' representative. Why on earth do you have to invite those cockroaches for coffee?

Magdalena   Did you give your daughter your storage room key?

Amparo   What storage room?

Magdalena   Yours.

Amparo   Why do you say that?

Magdalena *does not answer.*

Amparo   Listen, Magdalena, you better start being honest. You're making me nervous

Magdalena   Answer me. Did you give it to her or not?

Amparo   Why do you care whether I gave my daughter the key to my storage room?

Magdalena   I believe it's her.

Amparo   Who? What?

Magdalena   Your daughter, Amparo – the homeless with the blanket.

Amparo   Are you out of your mind? What have you been drinking this morning?

Magdalena   Just listen to me.

Amparo   You want me to listen to you?

Magdalena   Yes! Listen to me!

Amparo   I can't believe it. Every time something happens in the building – a door is forced, a fire extinguisher disappears – my daughter is the first person that pops into your mind. What would Marina be doing down there, hidden under a blanket? Tell me, why would she? Because I really do not get it.

Magdalena   Probably the same thing she's done up here, but now she's doing it in your storage room.

Amparo   Marina has changed as you know better than anybody. She's not a child anymore. She's a woman.

Magdalena   Yes, a woman. A woman who drinks until she falls flat on her face and uses drugs, every single day. And now she's moved in with a man thirty years older who neither you nor your husband knows.

Amparo   Look, I'm not slapping you only because it's Christmas, but let me tell you, right now, I'd like to slap you so hard that your face would stay warm for hours. Here I was, quietly doing my crosswords, and you had to show up and fuck up my whole day.

Magdalena   That's how you thank me?

Amparo   Thank you for what?

Magdalena   I saw this coming. I am way too good.

Amparo   I don't know if you saw it coming because you're too good, but you're definitely good at putting your nose in other people's business. This is a very large building – lots of people live here – and let me tell you again – Marina has changed.

Magdalena   Well, maybe I should have gone directly to the police and ignored you two, you and your daughter.

Amparo   I'm sure that when you die, you will be offered the whole of heaven. Your heart is so big it really doesn't fit in your chest.

Magdalena   Then, what? Will you answer me or not?

Amparo *does not answer.*

Magdalena   Did you or did you not give your daughter your storage room key?

Amparo   Marina is fully rehabilitated. *Fully* rehabilitated. How many times do I have to repeat it?

Magdalena   Nobody is ever *fully* rehabilitated. Don't be naive.

Amparo   Marina was.

Magdalena   You know better than anyone that it would not be the first time she stops using and then starts all over again.

Amparo   Why don't you just go fuck yourself? Do the world a favour.

Magdalena   Your tongue is dirtier than the chest of a snake – you know that, don't you?

Amparo   And you are out of your damn mind.

Magdalena   Move your ass and find that key!

Amparo *walks to a chest of drawers and starts rummaging for the key.*
Magdalena *paces the room.*

Magdalena   This apartment is always so unkempt, and you are such a mess that I doubt you can find it.

Amparo   If I find it, I'll shove it down your throat. No kidding.

Magdalena *rubs a finger on the furniture and checks it for dust.*
Amparo *keeps looking for the key.*

Magdalena   Before your mother moves in, you might think about cleaning this whole apartment a bit.

Amparo   Nope. Eusebio does not want her to move in.

Magdalena   What are you going to do?

Amparo   I don't know. But he says that if his mother died alone in her own house, why does mine have to die in ours, surrounded by family?

Magdalena   He's not completely wrong.

Amparo *stops, looks at* **Magdalena** *and remains pensive*

Amparo   She is in very bad shape. Her legs, her arms, her hands – she looks shocking. Her mind is sharp – she remembers every little thing – but her body is wasted.

Magdalena   Sad to end like this. She's suffered so much and now –

Amparo   If you could see her eyes when she looks at you from her bed, it's devastating. My heart breaks every time I enter her room. She was such a wicked woman, and, boy, was she a handful, that asshole. But since she got sick, her face radiates tenderness as if she never caused a single problem, that bitch.

Magdalena   Old people have to die, Amparo. It's a law of nature. From now on, you need to clear your head and start living your own life. You have enough to deal with.

Amparo   The only way I can enjoy life is to open the fridge and empty it out.

Magdalena   I really don't know where you put it all, to be honest. You should be the size of a gorilla given how much you devour, and look at you.

Amparo   My nerves are killing me and all the worries that prevent me from sleeping.

Magdalena   At least you have your daughter. Me – once God decides my time is up, no one will come and take care of me.

Amparo   Don't be pessimistic now!

Magdalena   What do you want me to do? I am a haunted soul just wandering from place to place.

Amparo   Why don't you do crossword puzzles?

Magdalena   Because I don't like them; I've told you many times.

Amparo   Have you ever tried to do one?

Magdalena   Puzzles, riddles, they aren't my thing, you know that.

Amparo   If you told me that you hate sudokus, word wheels, word searches, I would understand, but it makes no sense to me that you hate crossword puzzles in general –

Magdalena   Well, tough. I just don't like them. If I play anything, it has to be with a team, but playing by myself? I hate it.

Amparo   You certainly love your bingo! You're never bored at bingo.

Magdalena   Because bingo is a team game.

Amparo   A team game? Where's the team? Someone calls out the number, and the other crosses it on the sheet.

Magdalena   No, we always go fifty-fifty.

She crosses her arms and starts to rub them with the palm of her hands.

Shit, it's freezing in this house!

Amparo   Where did I put that damn key?

Magdalena   Is your heat on?

Amparo   Why? Are you cold?

Magdalena   I'm not cold. I'm freezing!

Amparo   I have everything on – the heating and the heater both.

Magdalena   Maybe it's just me. I'm out of sorts.

Amparo *pours two shots from a liquor bottle, and they chug them.*

Amparo   Do you think they suspect something?

Magdalena   What? Why would you say that? Because of the water?

Amparo   Because of the water, the bleach, the silicone in the keyhole and everything else.

Magdalena   Well, we've always been very careful not to get caught, always doing it at a reasonable hour, haven't we?

Amparo *lowers her head and places her hand on her neck.*

Magdalena   What's the matter?

Amparo   Nothing, something on my back itches, and I'm not sure what it is.

Magdalena   Let me take a look.

Amparo   I hope I didn't pick up a bug in there!

Magdalena   It's the sweater tag, not a bug!

Amparo   I thought I'd cut it off.

Magdalena   Maybe there were several. Hand me some scissors.

Amparo   Whatever, forget it.

Magdalena   Do you want me to cut it or not?

Amparo   No, don't cut it.

Magdalena   I thought you had said it was bothering you.

Amparo   Yes, but it doesn't matter.

Magdalena   Girl, you are a total mess.

Amparo   Well, I was thinking I might take it back and exchange it.

Magdalena   What's wrong? You don't like it anymore?

Amparo   No, not that. I think it might be a little too –

Magdalena   A little too what?

Silence. **Amparo** *puts her hands on her hips, elbows akimbo.*

Amparo   Magdalena, do you think I do too many colours?

Magdalena   Why do you ask me that?

Amparo   Don't lie to me, just tell me the truth.

Magdalena   Don't be ridiculous. You never tell your friend the truth.

Amparo   And why not?

Magdalena   Because it's disrespectful, tacky. Since when have we ever told each other the truth?

Amparo   Eusebio, this morning, before leaving for work, took a look at me and told me that I looked like a colourful couch.

Magdalena   You see? Nothing good comes from telling the truth.

Amparo   You think the same thing, don't you?

Magdalena   I didn't say that.

Amparo   So what *did* you say?

Magdalena   Come on, Amparo. He was pulling your leg. You know how he is.

Amparo   Nope, he wasn't kidding. He was completely serious.

Magdalena   If he was serious, you can tell him to fuck off.

Amparo   I think Eusebio doesn't like me anymore.

Magdalena   Please don't start with that again.

Amparo   He now says that I suffer from *horror vacui* syndrome and should go see a doctor.

Magdalena   What's that?

Amparo   Fear of emptiness or something like that.

Magdalena   What emptiness?

Amparo   No idea, but I think it is a serious illness.

Magdalena   Is it contagious?

Amparo   I don't know, but apparently more people are now afflicted with it.

Magdalena   Where did he get that from?

Amparo   Internet.

Magdalena   I wouldn't trust anything that's on the internet. It's making people crazy. It's the real sickness.

Amparo He says that I should be on it. That I should be doing all my crossword puzzles online. At least I wouldn't spend all that money on crossword magazines.

Magdalena Don't pay any attention to Eusebio. You're already hooked on turrón and crossword puzzles. God save us if you get hooked on the internet. Don't exchange the sweater, and don't connect to internet.

Amparo *reaches for the bottle.*

Amparo One day, if I'm fed up, I'll do something big that the whole world will know about. You better remember it.

Magdalena *holds out her glass while* **Amparo** *pours herself another shot.*

Magdalena Come on, pour me some.

Amparo *fills* **Magdalena**'s *glass.* **Magdalena** *shivers.*

Magdalena Damn it, I'm freezing!

Amparo Do like I do.

She chugs the alcohol.

You won't feel the cold, trust me.

Magdalena You're crazy!

Amparo If only you knew!

Magdalena, *glass in hand, walks to the window and looks outside.*

Magdalena Amparo, what's all this?

Amparo *joins her.*

Magdalena What's going on out there?

Amparo I'm not sure. It started descending, and it never went away. It looks as if they had set the streets on fire.

Magdalena Or put us all in a cauldron.

Amparo On TV, they just said they're not sure where it's coming from or if it will leave anytime soon.

Magdalena I've never seen such a dense fog in my whole life.

Amparo Earlier, I stepped outside to go to the bakery, but I had to turn right around and come back up. You couldn't see a soul. The street looked like a cemetery, and car beams looked like candles on the tombs of dead people. It's incredible what's going on in the sky. Last night, it was bursting with stars, and today, dark as the mouth of a wolf. As if someone had decided to pave it with asphalt while we were sleeping. God cannot be aware of what's going on down here if He is on the other side. Hell is slowly encroaching on Earth while the sky is blindfolded.

Magdalena   Amparo, what's going on?

Amparo   I don't know.

Silence.

But I've had the same recurring dream for weeks now. Every night, I dream that I'm pregnant. They take me to the hospital, and I give birth to a baby girl. When they hand her to me, I look at her and realize it's not a baby girl but – something else. Something that resembles Marina but actually is not.

Silence.

Sometimes I think about it. I don't feel like I gave birth to a baby girl but to a stone or a ball. A ball that has been abandoned on the floor since the day it was born. A ball that everyone constantly kicks around.

Magdalena   Someday, you and your daughter will realize everything I've done for you two, and then you'll thank me.

Amparo *stops looking outside and looks at* **Magdalena***.*

Amparo   Come to think of it – I think I did give it to her.

Magdalena   What?

Amparo   The storage room key, to Marina. She needed to put some things down there, and I gave it to her. It just dawned on me in a flash.

Magdalena *stares at* **Amparo** *silently.*

Amparo   You said five p.m., didn't you?

Magdalena *walks towards the door.*

Magdalena   Yes, you take care of the cake and just come up before five. I'll take care of the coffee.

Amparo   What should I bake?

Magdalena*, at the threshold, stops and looks at* **Amparo** *again.*

Amparo   What kind of cake should I bake?

Magdalena   Just bake whatever you want. Just put some whipped cream or meringue on top, and you're done. Don't waste your time.

Amparo *gets close to* **Magdalena** *and holds her hand.*

Amparo   Don't you worry about anything. I'll be there with you.

Magdalena *shuts the door.* **Amparo** *is left alone in her living room. With a lost gaze, she grabs the remote control and, mechanically and almost unconsciously, turns on the TV. The news is over; now they are broadcasting something like a Christmas concert, and a choir sings Mykola Leontovych's 'Carol of the Bells'.* **Amparo** *seizes the blanket she was using to cover her legs before* **Magdalena** *arrived and throws it over her shoulders like a cloak. She takes the ends and wraps herself tight. She exits the room as 'Carol of the Bells' keeps playing.*

In the basement, **Xiaomei** *and* **Ms Wang** *walk out of the apartment to the staircase.*

On the tenth floor, **Magdalena** *prepares the table for the birthday party – a tablecloth and some plates. Both the layout and decoration of the apartment suggest the sixties: a cross on the wall, a little Spanish flag, crocheted rugs and sad-looking furniture. The phone table holds a pile of unopened letters and a framed photo of her with her husband. In one corner, the Christmas tree is better decorated than* **Amparo**'s.

Amparo *leaves her fifth-floor apartment, carrying a cake down the corridor to the elevator.*

Ms Wang, *at the foot of the stairs, grabs her daughter's arm, and they begin to climb slowly, step by step.*

Magdalena, *on the tenth floor, continues the party preparations.*

Amparo *takes the elevator up to the tenth.*

Xiaomei *and her mother slowly climb the stairs from the basement to the ground-floor hallway.*

Magdalena, *on the tenth floor, places a coffee cup on each plate and, next to the plates, a teaspoon.*

Amparo *exits the elevator with the cake and walks to* **Magdalena**'s *door.*

Xiaomei *and her mother take the elevator to the tenth floor.*

Magdalena, *on the tenth floor, places a pile of napkins and a jug of water in the centre of the table.* **Amparo** *rings the doorbell;* **Magdalena** *opens the door;* **Amparo** *enters and hands* **Magdalena** *the cake, which* **Magdalena** *takes to the kitchen. The elevator opens.* **Ms Wang** *and* **Xiaomei** *walk down the corridor towards* **Magdalena**'s *flat.* **Xiaomei** *rings the doorbell. Inside,* **Amparo** *and* **Magdalena** *look at the clock,* *which strikes five.* **Magdalena** *looks at* **Amparo***; **Amparo** gives* **Magdalena** *the nod, and the latter walks to the door and opens it.*

Paradise

Magdalena *and* **Amparo** *on one side of the door and* **Xiaomei** *and* **Ms Wang** *on the other look at each other briefly, without a word. A strange, awkward silence.*

Magdalena   Please come in. Don't stay by the door.

Ms Wang*, holding her daughter's arm, enters the apartment.* **Magdalena** *walks to the table. She waits for* **Xiaomei** *and her mother then immediately invites them to take a seat. Mother and daughter sit down and look around.* **Amparo***, who has not moved, observes the scene from the door, which is still wide open.*

Ms Wang   这个地方太惬意了，是不是？/ Zhège dìfāng tài qièyì le, shìbúshì?[13]

Xiaomei   嗯，挺漂亮一个房子。/ Ng, tǐng piàoliàng yī gè fángzǐ.[14]

Ms Wang   她们看起来也特别好亲近。/ Tāmen kàn qǐlái yě tèbié hǎo qīnjìn.[15]

Xiaomei   我们搬家来这座楼住的第一天，这些这么友好的邻居就来敲我们的门请 我们吃午餐，这难道不是件幸运的事？/ Women bānjiā lái zhè zuò lóu zhù de dì yī tiān, zhè xiē zhème yòu hǎo de línjū jiù lái qiāo wǒmen de mén qǐng wǒmen chī wǔcān, zhè nán dào bú shì jiàn xìngyùn de shì ma?[16]

Ms Wang   是的，很幸运。/ Shì de, hěn xìngyùn.[17]

Xiaomei *and* **Ms Wang** *look at their neighbours and smile.*

Magdalena   Let me go get the coffee. I'll be right back.

She goes to the kitchen, and **Xiaomei** *and* **Ms Wang** *look at* **Amparo***, who is still standing by the open apartment door. Silence.* **Xiaomei** *takes*

---

13 What a beautiful apartment, isn't it?
14 Yes, it is very pretty.
15 And they seem so nice!
16 Aren't we lucky to have such kind neighbours, who come to our place and invite us for coffee?
17 Yes, we certainly are.

another look at the house. **Magdalena** *appears holding a tray with a coffee maker, two cream pitchers and a sugar bowl.*

Magdalena   Amparo, honey, come and help me set up.

Amparo *closes the door and walks to the table. She takes the tray from* **Magdalena**'s *hands.*

Amparo   Let me serve you. (*To* **Xiaomei**.) Black or with milk?

Xiaomei   With milk, please.

Amparo   How would you like your milk?

Xiaomei   Warm, if possible.

Amparo (*to* **Magdalena**)   Do we have warm milk?

Magdalena   Yes, in the other creamer.

Amparo *grabs the warm milk creamer and pours it for* **Xiaomei**.

Amparo (*to* **Xiaomei**)   What about your mother?

Xiaomei   Same for her, thank you.

Amparo *pours the coffee from east to west, or right to left.*

Ms Wang   非常感谢。/ Fēicháng gǎnxiè.[18]

Xiaomei   Thank you.

Amparo   The usual, Magdalena.

Magdalena   Yes, the usual.

Amparo *serves coffee to* **Magdalena**. **Magdalena** *puts the sugar bowl in the middle of the table.*

Magdalena   Serve yourself sugar.

Xiaomei   We like it bitter.

Magdalena *grabs the sugar bowl and puts at least seven teaspoons in her cup.*

Magdalena   I certainly don't. I put sugar in mine, a lot of sugar. If I don't, I think it tastes like a sewer, although, even with sugar, it still tastes like crap.

---

18 Thank you very much.

With her teaspoon, she stirs the massive amount of sugar in her coffee.

I actually don't know why I still drink coffee.

Amparo *serves herself some coffee and sits down. As if in a duel, the four women lift their coffee cups and sip at the same time. Silence.*

Xiaomei   Okay then, what can we chat about?

Silence.

I mean, we should be chatting about something, right?

Amparo *and* **Magdalena** *look at each other, not knowing what to say.*

Xiaomei   Do you know any jokes?

Silence.

I know one. I'm not sure if you'll think it's funny, but it's the only one that comes to mind. Okay, here I go. What's the difference between someone from China and a plate full of shit?

Silence.

Between a Chinese person and plate full of shit, what do you think is the difference?

Nobody says anything.

The plate!

Nobody laughs.

The difference is the plate.

Xiaomei *laughs out loud.*

Pretty good, isn't it?

Silence.

You didn't think it was funny?

Nobody answers.

Okay, here comes another one. A Spaniard, a Frenchman, an Englishman and a Chinese man are on a plane. All of a sudden, the plane begins to shudder. The pilot comes out and says to the four passengers: 'I'm sorry, but one of you has to jump.' The Englishman stands up and says, 'I – for England, Big Ben and beer – I throw myself headfirst'. And he jumps. The plane stabilizes but, after fifteen minutes or so, starts making strange noises again. The pilot comes out and tells the three remaining passengers, 'I'm sorry, but one of you has to jump', and the Frenchman says, 'I – for France, the Eiffel Tower and the Bastille – I will throw myself out', and he jumps out. The plane stabilizes but, after half an hour or so, starts to shudder. The pilot comes out of the cockpit and says to the two remaining passengers, 'I'm sorry, but one of you has to jump'. And the Spaniard says, 'I – for Spain, Real Madrid FC and wine – go fuck yourself, Chinaman'.

Amparo *and* **Magdalena** *look at each other silently.*

Xiaomei   Now, seriously. If my mother gets close to a neighbour's dog and pets it, it's not because she wants to eat it. She just loves animals, and she's just petting it. I hope you understand the difference, or do you really believe everything that's said about us?

Silence.

That thing about our dead, for example. The urban legend that we never bury our dead. What do you think, true or false?

Magdalena   Listen, let me tell you something –

Xiaomei   Do you think we bury them? Yes or no. Answer.

Amparo *and* **Magdalena** *look at each other silently. They are embarrassed.*

Amparo (*suddenly, shouting*)   True!

Magdalena   What?

Xiaomei   Nope, not true. It is a lie. For example, my father is still sitting on a chair downstairs in the basement, but he is inside the freezer.

Amparo *and* **Magdalena** *are shocked.*

Xiaomei   But not the freezer in the kitchen, another one. We have three: one for the veggies, one for the doggies that we pick up on the street and, in the third one, my father.

Silence.

Magdalena (*to* **Amparo**)   Go, hurry, and bring the cake.

Amparo *gets up, goes to the kitchen.*

Xiaomei   I was six years old, and I remember it was also Christmas. My mother and I were on a crosswalk. Apparently, the driver didn't see her and got extremely close. My mother fell to the ground, and the car almost ran her over. Normally, the driver would have stopped. Instead, the driver accelerated and disappeared. No one could recognize the driver, but I always knew that you were the one driving the car, the one who puts pins in the locks and the one who tells these jokes. Who do you think I learned them from?

Magdalena *does not answer.*

Xiaomei Through the inner courtyard, I have been hearing you making fun of us for years. What have my mother and I done for you to treat us so badly?

Amparo *appears carrying the cake.*

Amparo Should I turn down the lights, light the candle, or how should we do this?

Magdalena *gets up.*

Magdalena Here, give it to me.

Magdalena *takes the cake from* **Amparo** *and puts it on the table while smiling at* **Ms Wang**.

Magdalena Happy birthday.

Amparo Happy birthday.

Xiaomei (*to* **Ms Wang**) 大家说很高兴也很荣幸你能和她们一起住在这座楼里，成为她们的新邻居。/ Dà jiā shuō hěn gāoxìng yě hěn róngxìng nǐ néng hé tāmen yī qǐ zhù zài zhè zuò lóu lǐ, chéngwéi tāmen de xīn línjū.[19]

Ms Wang 这正是我要说的。/ Zhè zhèng shì wǒ yào shuō de.[20] (*To* **Magdalena**.) 谢谢。/ Xiè xiè.[21] (*To* **Amparo**.) 非常感谢。/ Fēi cháng gǎn xiè.[22]

Magdalena Amparo, the candle.

Amparo Huh?

Magdalena Light it up.

---

19 They say that it is wonderful that you live in the building with them and that they are honoured to be your neighbour.
20 An honour for me, too.
21 Thank you.
22 Thank you very much.

Amparo   Do you have a lighter?

Magdalena   Take these matches.

Amparo   Okay.

She takes the matchbook and drags a match along the striker, but it does not catch fire. She tries again, unsuccessfully.

It won't light.

Magdalena *takes the matchbook from her.*

Magdalena   Let me do it.

She tries to light it.

Well, I can't light it either.

Amparo   It's because of the fog. It's so humid not even cars can start.

Magdalena   Go to the kitchen and bring a lighter.

Amparo *finds a lighter near an ashtray nearby and hands it to* **Magdalena**.

Amparo   That's not necessary. Here's one.

With determination, **Magdalena** *takes the lighter and lights the candle.*

Xiaomei (*to* **Ms Wang**)   许个愿。/ Xǔ gè yuàn.[23]

Ms Wang   因为今天 我的生日？/ Yīn wéi jīntiān shì wǒ de shēngrì?[24]

Xiaomei   你不记得了吗？/ Nǐ bú jì dé le ma?[25]

Ms Wang *tries to remember.*

Xiaomei   最终看到她们拿阿司匹林当借口 下楼来，实际上那时她们想的是让你 上 去， 给你一个节日惊喜。/ Zuì zhōng kàn dào tāmen ná āsīpǐlín dāng jièkǒu xià lóu lái, shíjìshàng nà shí tāmen xiǎng de shì ràng nǐ shàng qù, gěi nǐ yī gè jiérì jīngxǐ.[26]

Ms Wang   那这节日惊喜太令人开心了。我想她们从未这样做过。/ Nà zhè jié rì jīng xǐ tài lìng rén kāi xīn le. Wǒ xiǎng tāmen cóng wèi zhè yàng zuò guò.[27]

---

23 Make a wish!
24 Today's my birthday?
25 Did you forget?
26 Actually, they came down with the aspirin excuse, but what they really wanted was to invite us to their apartment for a surprise birthday party.
27 That's so wonderful. I think it is my first ever surprise birthday party.

Xiaomei   想好你的生日愿望没有？/ Xiǎng hǎo nǐ de shēngrì yuànwàng méi yǒu?[28]

Ms Wang *thinks about it.*

Ms Wang   想好了。/ Xiàng hǎo le.[29]

Xiaomei   现在吹吧。/ Xiànzài chuī ba.[30]

Ms Wang *blows out the candle, and* **Xiaomei** *applauds.* **Magdalena** *and* **Amparo** *watch the whole scene without participating.*

Xiaomei   许愿了吗？/ Xǔyuàn le ma?[31]

Ms Wang   恩，许了。/ ēn, xǔ le.[32]

Xiaomei   这蛋糕真好看啊。你不觉得吗？/ Zhè dàngāo zhēn hǎokàn a. nǐ bù juédé ma?[33]

Ms Wang   恩， 漂亮。/ Ēn piàoliàng.[34]

With the Christmas tree lights flashing, **Amparo** *and* **Magdalena** *stare at* **Ms Wang** *sitting at the table in front of the birthday cake.*

Xiaomei   My mother says that you are wonderful women and that the party is great.

She takes a knife from the table and stands up. They all look at her in silence.

Okay, hand us your dishes because we are about to serve you.

Everybody, except **Ms Wang***, passes her plate, and* **Xiaomei** *divides the cake.*

Xiaomei   The first piece for my mother because it is her birthday. (*To* **Ms Wang***.*) 第一块是给你的， 妈妈， 把盘子拿她这儿来。/ Dìyī kuài shì gěi nǐde māma, bǎ pánzi ná tā zhèr lái.[35]

Ms Wang *does what her daughter says, and* **Xiaomei** *places the first piece on her mother's plate.*

---

28 Did you make your wish?
29 Yes.
30 Then blow out the candle.
31 Did you make a wish?
32 Yes, I did.
33 What a pretty cake, don't you think?
34 Yes, it is wonderful.
35 The first one is for you, Mom. Hand me your plate.

Ms Wang (*to* **Magdalena**)   谢谢，非常感谢。/ Xièxiè fēicháng gǎnxiè.[36]

Xiaomei *cuts another slice.*

Xiaomei   The second piece – for the neighbour on the fifth floor.

She puts the slice on **Amparo** *'s plate.*

Xiaomei   You get the third piece.

She cuts another slice and puts it on **Magdalena** *'s plate.*

Xiaomei   And this one for me.

She puts a piece on her plate and sits down.

请慢用。/ Qǐng màn yòng.[37]

Ms Wang   请慢用。/ Qǐng màn yòng.[38]

Xiaomei   Bon appétit.

Magdalena   Bon appétit.

Amparo   Bon appétit.

The four take their spoons at the same time. Before digging in, they look at each other defiantly. At the same time, they cut off a bite with their spoons, take it to their respective mouths and chew it.

Magdalena   Well, then. We've done our part. Now, it's your turn.

Suddenly, everything goes pitch black.

What's that?

Amparo   Seems like the power went out.

Magdalena *gets up.*

Magdalena   Let me go check. Stay here.

Magdalena *exits.* **Amparo**, **Xiaomei** *and* **Ms Wang** *stay in the living room.*

Xiaomei (*to* **Ms Wang**)   她们在看发生了什 么事。/ Tāmen zài kàn fāshēng le shénme shì.[39]

---

36 Thank you, thank you very much.
37 *Bon appétit.*
38 *Bon appétit.*
39 They are checking what went wrong.

Ms Wang   又是我的生日吗？ / Yòu shì wǒ de shēngrì ma?[40]

Xiaomei   对， 我想她们是要再给你一个惊喜。 / Duì, wǒ xiǎng tāmen shì yào zài gěi nǐ yī gè jīngxǐ.[41]

Magdalena *enters.*

Magdalena   The fuse didn't blow. Phone a neighbour; the power should be out all over the building. I'll go get some candles. Don't move.

She exits again.

Amparo   Who should I call? I'm not speaking to any of our neighbours.

She grabs the phone and the pile of letters next to it falls down.

Damn it – great timing.

She kneels and, while holding the phone, starts gathering all the letters.

Magdalena *comes back with a flashlight and several candles.*

Magdalena   Don't worry about that. I should have put them somewhere else, but I always forget.

Amparo   Why do you have so many letters?

Magdalena   From the bank. They are relentless.

Amparo   Why don't you open them?

Magdalena   I never find the time. And with everything going on around these dates, I always forget.

Having picked up all the letters, **Amparo** *gets up.*

Amparo   Where do you want me to put them?

Magdalena   Same place they were.

She puts the flashlight on the table as if it were a lamp and starts giving candles out.

Come on, help me with the candles.

Amparo *gives the lighter to* **Magdalena**, *who lights a pair of candles and passes them to her neighbours.*

---

40 Is it my birthday again?
41 Yes, I think they might give you another surprise.

Magdalena   Here.

The neighbours take the lighter from **Magdalena** *and light their respective candles which they place around the living room.* **Magdalena** *grabs the phone from* **Amparo**.

Magdalena   Give it to me. I'll make the calls.

She dials a number, and **Ms Wang** *pretends to dial an imaginary phone.*

Magdalena   What is she doing?

They all stare at **Ms Wang**, *who starts to laugh.*

Xiaomei   She's imitating you. When she imitates someone, it's because she likes that person or because she is very happy.

Magdalena   Hello, Rosa? Yes, Magdalena here, from the tenth floor. My power just went out, and I wanted to know if – Okay. No, the fuse didn't blow; everything seems fine. Okay, then. I'm not sure what's going on. No, no, don't you worry about a thing. Yes, that's right. Bye, then. And thank you. Yes, yes. Goodbye.

She hangs up and thinks.

Xiaomei   By the way, I still haven't introduced myself. I am Xiaomei, but I changed my name to Estrella when I started attending school.

Silence.

Do you like my name?

Magdalena   Look, this is getting complicated. The power is out; your mother has already had two slices of cake and you still haven't told us anything.

Amparo   Yes, that's right. Will you tell us what you have to tell us or leave us hanging here until your mother finishes the whole cake.

Xiaomei *looks at* **Magdalena** *and addresses her.*

Xiaomei   As soon as you tell me that you are ready.

Silence.

Are you?

Amparo *looks at* **Magdalena**, *but she does not answer.*

Xiaomei   Are you ready or not?

Magdalena *does not answer.* **Amparo** *looks at her, worried.*

Amparo   What's the matter with you? She's asking you. Why aren't you answering her?

Xiaomei   Because she does not know if she is.

Amparo, *not fully understanding what's going on, looks at* **Xiaomei**.

Amparo   What doesn't she know?

Xiaomei   This morning I told her, 'You remind me a lot of Lord Ye', the man who loved dragons so much and had them painted all over his house, but she didn't let me finish the story.

Amparo   What story are you talking about?

Xiaomei   A story about a man who really loves dragons. He loves them so much that the news spreads far and wide until one day, even the king of dragons learns about it. Upon hearing the story, the king of dragons decides to visit the man who so adores dragons. There is a problem, though. He is so big, he can't get through Lord Ye's door, so he tries to look inside the house through the window. But when Lord Ye sees that huge head so close to him and so real, he is terrified and runs away and never wants to hear about dragons again in his life.

Magdalena   Again with that fairy tale?

Xiaomei   It's not a fairy tale, it's a proverb.

Magdalena   I don't care. If you're trying to confuse us, I am sorry to say you won't get away with it.

Xiaomei   I am definitely not trying to confuse you. On the contrary, I am trying to tell you something, but you just keep interrupting me, and I can never finish.

Magdalena   Just finish it, for God's sake! What do you want to tell me?

Xiaomei   That both you and Lord Ye are afraid of learning the truth, even if you pretend not to be.

Magdalena   Me? Afraid?

Xiaomei   Yes.

Amparo   Start talking. Is it my daughter? Or who the hell is the homeless person under the blanket

Xiaomei   No, it is not your daughter.

Amparo   Really?

Xiaomei   Yes.

Magdalena   Who is it then?

Xiaomei *points to the framed picture next to the small table with the phone and the letters.*

Xiaomei   Exactly that one.

Amparo *and* **Magdalena** *look towards the small table, not understanding anything.*

Xiaomei   The man in the picture.

Amparo   It can't be the man in the picture because the man in the picture is her husband, and he's been on an international business trip for the last two weeks.

Ms Wang *gets up, cuts herself another slice of cake and starts eating it.*

Magdalena   Yes, it can't be my husband. You must be confused.

Xiaomei   Your husband hasn't gone anywhere, and you know it perfectly well. Your husband was let go from his job a long time ago, but he never dared to tell you. He pretends to go to work every day. A few weeks ago, he couldn't handle it anymore. He made up the story about the trip and locked himself up in the storage room.

Amparo *looks at* **Magdalena**.

Xiaomei   I think the police, with some people from the bank, will be around shortly to seize your apartment.

Silence.

According to what your husband told me, he tried to explain it to you several times. But you paid him no mind. Same way you are doing with the proverb about Lord Ye and the dragons. At least if you had been brave enough to open one of those letters, you would have found out for yourself. Business trips are rare at these times. The power doesn't go out unless fuses blow but – I already told you that you and Lord Ye are very much alike.

Magdalena *says nothing.*

Xiaomei   However, you don't have to worry at all because I can lend you a hand. I want to help you and your husband.

Magdalena *still does not say anything.*

Xiaomei   This is my offer: if you don't have another place to go, you can stay in my apartment.

Silence.

Down there. In the basement. I would move up here with my mother. I have already spoken with the bank, and they are fine with it. I will take care of all your debt and the mortgage, too. I won't charge you anything for staying in the basement. But of course in exchange, you would help me out with the beer business. You help me, and I help you. What do you think?

Silence.

Your husband agrees with me. He thinks it's a good idea. But we still do not know what you think about it.

Magdalena *goes towards the framed picture, grabs it and stares at it. She raises her head and looks into the void.*

Xiaomei   Oh, and Merry Christmas, by the way.

Magdalena *lets the framed picture fall, and it crashes into pieces.* **Amparo** *backs towards the door. She exits the apartment, leaving* **Magdalena** *alone with the Chinese women.*

Xiaomei   And no need to thank me, if you do not want to. After all, we are neighbours, and what are neighbours for if not helping each other out?

Magdalena *looks at* **Xiaomei**.

Xiaomei   Right?

Magdalena *exits her apartment and runs to the elevator, but* **Amparo** *is using it to descend to the fifth floor. With determination,* **Magdalena** *grabs the railing and starts running from the tenth floor to the basement.* **Xiaomei**, *still in the living room, closes the door and starts to clear the table: she removes the dishes, shakes out the tablecloth and takes everything to the kitchen.* **Amparo**, *who has already reached the fifth floor, enters her home, sits down in her armchair and grabs her crossword magazine.* **Xiaomei**, *on the tenth floor, starts to rearrange the furniture, putting the couch in front of the window. She helps her mother get comfortable.*

Magdalena, *who has just arrived in the basement, clumsily moves through the corridors as if she were an insect trapped in a glass jar. Curiously, her hair no longer resembles that of the queens engraved on a* *coin. Now it looks more like a withered flower or a deflated air-mattress. Distraught, she stops in front of a chipped door. She looks for a doorbell but can't find one, so she knocks and waits, but no one answers. She knocks again and, suddenly, it opens by itself, but there is no one, only darkness.*

Xiaomei, *on the tenth floor, sits on the couch next to her mother.* **Amparo**, *on the fifth floor, with the magazine in her hand, looks absent minded.*

Magdalena, *in the basement, stops in front of her storage-room door, knocks and waits. But no one opens.* **Magdalena** *knocks on the door once more and, suddenly, it opens by itself, but there is nothing there, only darkness.* **Magdalena** *walks into the storage room. A haunting, telluric/eerie sound – a mixture of chimes, wind and fire – rumbles like a cloud of millions of bumblebees far away.* **Magdalena** *looks for a switch, flips it and the storage room light comes on. Hanging from the ceiling is a rope from which a man wrapped in a blanket is hanging.* **Magdalena** *screams in horror, and the scream rises from the basement to the top floor.* **Xiaomei**, *sitting next to her mother, watches the sky through the window.* **Amparo**, *in her fifth-floor flat, covers her ears then turns on the TV.*

TV News   The strange fog formation we have been experiencing since the first of the year persists. Temperatures drop in this atypical, but no longer surprising weather phenomenon. The grey ocean continues to expand at full speed. The Meteorological Agency continues to warn about the danger the reduced visibility caused by this unusual and persistent phenomenon poses for many. It is estimated that, today, more than a third of the population has begun to suffer symptoms of anxiety due to confusion: after so many days of fog, many citizens have begun to confuse nights with days and days with nights. Pending new data, and government directives, the ban on driving any type of vehicle is still on. The government spokesman announced this afternoon that they continue to investigate, but unfortunately, until the mysterious phenomenon subsides, the only thing we can do is get used to the darkness.

Xiaomei *and* **Ms Wang**, *lying on the couch, cover themselves with a blanket, turn off the lights and everything goes dark.*

TV News   Good night.
To be continued . . .

Lulú

To Andrea D'Odorico Agosto

Characters

Amancio
Calisto
Abelardo
Lulú
Julián
Woman

I

Amancio   The first time I saw her, she was at the base of an apple tree. She had a wound on her back. She was bare-chested, wearing nothing but tights. An unconscious woman, half-naked, lying on the grass. By that time, I had already turned into a sad and gloomy man. I would spend every morning denying that the sun was up, without a single reason to get out of bed. My wife had recently passed away, and, since then, my world was pointless. Nothing brought me any joy. Nothing could surprise me, and no matter how hard I tried, I failed to find anything worth living for. The doctor prescribed me pills, but I refused to take them because, deep down, I didn't want to get better. Suffering was my only source of comfort. It may seem strange but only pain and suffering eased my agony; and, of course, searching for the snake that killed my wife.

It happened on a Sunday. We were having lunch with our sons, lying on the grass, when, out of nowhere, that snake appeared. It quickly sank its fangs into my wife's throat. If the bite had been below the neck, she might've survived, but bites from the neck up are deadly. After a week in the hospital, she died. We held her vigil at our house. The next day, we buried her in the same place where, a few days earlier, that creature had bitten her – underneath the apple tree. I could've gone back inside to rest, or I could've stayed there, firmly rooted by her graveside, until I could finally convince myself of what had happened. Instead, right after her burial, I picked up an axe, set traps and started spreading poison everywhere. My only purpose in life was to find that creature and kill it. I forgot all my regular duties, and life completely centred on finding that creature – that snake, that snake and nothing but that snake. That's what my life has become – each day a sad repetition of the previous. Problems start when monotony takes over your life since it exhausts and desensitizes you. It desensitizes you to the point that, at any given moment, it is difficult to remember if you are still alive or if it's been a while since you took your last breath. Suddenly, you find yourself wandering around, just an empty shell of your former self. Because that's what I became – an empty shell who wouldn't eat, sleep or think about anything except finding that damn snake.

Calisto *and* **Abelardo**, **Amancio**'s *sons, enter.*

II

Calisto   Everything that you and Mum used to take care of –

Abelardo   – the pruning –

Calisto   – the harvest –

Abelardo   – the distribution –

Calisto   Abelardo and I will take care of it all.

Abelardo   And we aren't complaining. You know how much we love to work on the farm.

Calisto   But, Dad, like the way you've been forgetting the apple trees –

Abelardo   – both Calisto and me think you've forgotten us, too.

Pause.

Calisto   You probably think that this is absolutely normal –

Abelardo   – but it's far from normal for a man to spend his whole day with an axe in his hand, looking for a snake.

Calisto   Today, even before the sun came up, you were already wandering around the apple trees, and it's been dark for a while now.

Abelardo   Do you realize what this means?

There's no answer.

Calisto   It's been a while since you last ate –

Abelardo   It's been a while since you last slept –

Calisto   It's been a while since you last bathed –

Abelardo   And it's tough for us to see you like this because you say that you'll change –

Calisto   – but then you forget and ignore us.

Silence.

Abelardo   We don't like having to say this, but both Calisto and I hate our lives right now, so unless you do something to get out of your funk –

Calisto   – or we'll just pack up –

Abelardo   – gather our things –

Calisto   – and get out of here.

Calisto *and* **Abelardo** *exit.*

III

Amancio   Every night, back at home after looking for that snake, I would find my kids arguing about me in their bedroom. But instead of talking to them and reassuring them, I would always react the same way. I would get in my car and drive around for hours. Every time I get nervous, I always do the same thing. And that day was no different.

Pause.

It was pitch black. One of those nights when the fog gets so low, the sky seems to melt with the earth, and they become one. And I remember it clearly because I thought that it was dangerous to keep driving in that thick fog, that it was time to turn around and go back home as soon as possible. And then, while I was parking –

He sees something far away.

– the headlights shone on some strange bump right behind one of the trees.

Half-naked, in just stockings, with a wound on her back, a woman is lying on the floor.

A wounded animal was my first thought.

Amancio, *very slowly, starts walking towards said bump.*

But as I was getting closer, the fog vanished, I could see better –

He stops near the bump and observes it.

And I soon realized that it was not an animal; it was, in fact, a woman.

IV

Amancio *examines the woman without touching her. Then, to check for a reaction, he softly touches her with his foot, but the woman does not say or do anything.*

Excuse me, can you hear me?

He stoops to her level.

Miss, can you hear me?

The woman starts to move very slowly.

Are you all right?

Slowly, the woman turns over and sees **Amancio** *facing her. Then, she looks around.*

Lulú   What am I doing here?

Amancio   I don't know. I was parking my car, and I just happened to see you.

Lulú   Where are we?

Amancio   On my property – an apple orchard near the mountain.

Lulú   It hurts. What's the matter with me?

Amancio   A wound. You better not touch it. It could get infected.

Lulú *touches her back. Then she looks at her fingers and sees they're covered in blood.*

Lulú   What have you done to me?

Amancio   What do you mean?

Lulú *firmly presses her forehead with her hand.*

Lulú   Forgive me, but I can't remember anything. My head feels as if I just woke up after sleeping a hundred years.

Amancio   We'd better call an ambulance.

The woman does not respond.

Do you want me to take you to the hospital?

There's no answer.

You're probably lost and missing – people might be looking for you.

Lulú   Do you know what time it is?

Amancio   No, I don't have a watch, but it must be late. Or it might be very early, depending.

The woman looks around again.

It seems as if someone turned off the light, and the whole world has become night.

Amancio *realizes that the young woman is still half-naked. He takes off his jacket and hands it to her.*

Take my jacket. You must be freezing.

He helps the young woman to put on his jacket.

Perfect. It's too big for you, but at least it will warm you up.

The young woman, with **Amancio***'s jacket on her shoulders, starts walking around, disoriented in the fog. He follows her with his gaze.*

What's your name? Do you remember your name?

The young woman stops wandering, turns around and looks at **Amancio** *again.*

Or don't you even remember your name?

Pause.

Lulú   Yes, I do remember my name.

Silence.

My name's Lulú.

V

Amancio   The next thing I remember is opening my eyes in my bedroom and feeling a pounding headache. I was all alone in my bedroom. There wasn't anyone else. What happened, and how did I get here? Still obsessing about what might have happened the night before, I went to the bathroom, sank my head in the sink and while the cold stream of water was splashing the back of my neck I heard a strange sound in the background. I closed the faucet, walked towards the window and looked out, and I was shocked to see right across –

Pause.

– right across, surrounded by fruit and with her hair all laced with flowers, the woman I had found the night before under the apple tree.

VI

Abelardo *and* **Calisto** *appear, carrying a basket full of apples and a crown of flowers that they put on* **Lulú***'s head.*

Calisto   You might not realize it at first because they are, more or less, similar –

Abelardo   – but we grow up to eight different types of apples.

Calisto *grabs one of the apples.*

Calisto   We have one called Honeycrisp –

Abelardo *does the same with a different apple.*

Abelardo   Another called Granny Smith –

Calisto   We also have Red Delicious –

Abelardo   And McIntosh –

Calisto   And Golden –

Abelardo   And Gala –

Calisto   And Ambrosia –

Abelardo   And Fuji.

Lulú *observes the eight types of apples.*

Abelardo   These are the names of each variety. Some you eat raw –

Calisto   – others you use for cooking. . .

Abelardo   – and others to make cider.

Calisto   Do you like cider?

Abelardo   We make it ourselves.

Calisto   And you better believe that it is all natural.

Both young men smile and **Abelardo** *runs out from the porch.*

Lulú   Do you recognize them by just looking at them, or do you
mistake them sometimes?

Calisto   The apples?

Lulú   Yes –

She grabs one of the apples and shows it to **Calisto**.

Lulú   This one, for example, out of the eight varieties – which one
would you say it is?

Calisto   That's a Honeycrisp. It has a rather bitter taste –

Abelardo *runs back, carrying a glass bottle in his hand.*

Calisto– and it ripens during the first twenty days of October.

Abelardo *raises the bottle and shows it to* **Lulú**.

Abelardo   The cider!

Calisto   If you'd like, one day, we can go into the fields, and I'll let you taste each variety. They taste different right after being picked. Completely different. Do you like motorbikes?

There's no answer.

I have a motocross, a 125 cc, but I'm always replacing pieces. I would love to be a professional racer, you know? But, for now, I'm just racing on natural terrains and getting badly hurt on the mountain. All I can do, right now.

He takes off his shirt and shows **Lulú** *his chest.*

Calisto   Look, I have scars all over my body. I look like a road map.

Lulú *observes* **Calisto**'s *chest.*

Calisto   We could go for a ride, whenever you feel like it. What do you think?

Abelardo   I'd rather shoot birds. I take my shotgun, aim it at any bird resting on a branch and then I pull the trigger, and I shoot for the head. Boom! I kill them all. I can't ride a motorbike for shit, but I'm the best shooter there is. Birds mess everything up. They peck at the fruit and ruin it, so it's better to kill them all. Then I fry or grill them and eat them. Quails, blackbirds, sparrows, turtledoves, partridges, swifts, doves, goldfinches, hummingbirds – If you want me to, I'll kill whatever you prefer. You can eat any bird – they're all delicious. Have you ever tried them?

Lulú *looks at* **Amancio**, *who has not moved and has witnessed the whole scene.*

Lulú   What about you, Amancio? Do you like birds?

Pause.

Come join us. Get closer.

Amancio *gets closer to* **Lulú**.

Amancio   The oldest is Calisto and the younger, Abelardo. They're my sons. They started helping out, but now they run the business. Abelardo supervises the pruning and the harvest. Calisto, the numbers guy, is in charge of the payments. Right now, they know the farm better than I do, and even though they look like kids, they're very responsible.

Lulú   It truly is a beautiful place. It doesn't matter where you look –

She embraces **Amancio**.

– I don't know –

Pause.

– as if, all of a sudden, we fell through a hole, and arriving on the other side, we appeared in one of those fantasy stories you read to kids before they fall asleep.

VII

Amancio   A man only wants to find his life's meaning, or so they say. I had just found mine, and it was crystal clear that it was just a coincidence. According to my kids, the signs were obvious, and you had to be blind not to see it: Lulú was a gift from heaven; God put her in our path, and that's how we should interpret it. Amazing things can happen unexpectedly, and we'd just experienced it. Why not? Truth be told, we could have been suspicious of a woman who appeared out of nothing and becomes part of the family without any problem whatsoever. However, my kids and I had been through a very rough patch; we had suffered so much that we decided to move forward without asking too many questions. And now it was the time for answers. It had been pouring rain forever, and finally, one day –

VIII

Lulú   Finally, one day, the clouds disappear, and the sun shines again.

Amancio   Your name. I'd heard it before, but I had never met anyone with that name.

Lulú   No one has that name.

Amancio   Really?

Lulú   No. It's a nickname that several names share. They all start with 'Lu'. You need only to repeat the first syllable, Lu-Lu, and you can forget the rest. How far do they go?

Amancio   Huh?

Lulú   The apple trees. It seems as if there are lots of them.

Amancio   Over there, all the way down to the river and on the other side, half-way up the mountain.

He extends his hand out from the balcony and grabs an apple

Look, so you get an idea.

He pulls a knife out of his pocket, cuts the apple in half and shows one half to **Lulú**.

Amancio   If we observed the farm from the sky, bird's-eye view, and the inside of this apple was a map, the house would be where the seeds are, right here, in the centre. Check it out, it has the shape of a star, and we would be right inside the star, and all this yellow that surrounds it, the flesh of the fruit, that would be the apple field.

Lulú *stops looking at the apple, looks around again and points at something with her index finger.*

Lulú   What about that thing out there?

There's no response.

That red thing, with a cusp?

Amancio   That's a windmill.

Pause.

Well, it *was* a windmill because nobody used it, and now it stands abandoned. One day it broke down. and we decided to turn it into a hostel.

Lulú   You have a hostel inside the property?

Amancio   Yes, it helps our workers moneywise, and it's better for us because we can control the women better.

Lulú   The women? Why? Only women work the fields?

Amancio   The female hand is better than the male's for some tasks. Fruit is delicate, and you have to be very careful when picking it.

Lulú   How many women?

Amancio   Right around fifty. My kids handle all the contracts. It's been a while since I dealt with them. I only know that you'd better be careful with them. They're not particularly dangerous, but they are poor and uneducated. Once, when the kids were very young, they broke into the house and robbed us – we have bad memories from that day. They didn't hurt us, but they became violent, and we were scared. That's why we built the wire fence.

Lulú   What wire fence?

Amancio   It separates the house from the property.

Lulú   I didn't know there was a wire fence.

She squints.

Amancio   – I thought we'd already told you.

Lulú   Huh?

Amancio   Well, then, I'm telling you now – you'd be wise to stay on this side and never cross it. We already had an incident, and we don't want another.

Lulú *takes a picture from her breast and shows it to* **Amancio***.*

Lulú   She's very pretty. Who is she?

Amancio   Where did you get that from?

Lulú   I found it here, inside your jacket. Amancio. Hand it over.

Amancio *takes the picture from* **Lulú***'s hands and looks at it.*

Amancio   I met her in town years ago. We fell in love, got married and soon after the boys were born, we bought this property and planted all the trees. It was the great promise of our love: a field full of apple trees. The early years were tough, but bit by bit, things started looking better, and then, when we started doing great –

He stops looking at the picture and looks at the floor.

– she died, and the apple trees, my sons and I – we were devastated and felt very alone.

Silence.

Lulú   What happened to her?

Amancio *looks at* **Lulú***, and his expression changes.*

Amancio   A snake bit her.

His hands imitate claws, and he puts them on his throat.

Right here, on her throat. And a week later, she died.

Silence.

Once, I hit it with the axe and almost cut it in half. When I reached down to get it, it slipped out of my hands, and I haven't seen it since.

Lulú *gives* **Amancio** *a long, deep kiss on the mouth. She stops kissing him, and the two look at each other.*

Amancio   It's been a long time since I tasted such a sweet kiss.

Lulú   With me, you'll have whatever you want. Close your eyes and imagine you're a bee, and I'm a honeycomb overflowing with honey.

IX

Amancio   And that's exactly what I did: I turned into a bee, always flying towards her beehive. I drank all the nectar that I found on my way from the first to the last drop. And with my mouth full of honey, I grabbed her breasts. Two round and extremely soft breasts, like sugar, that became two white seagulls that spread their wings and started to fly high – so high that it gave me vertigo, scared me, overcame me to the point that I witnessed them turning from white to black and, in the end, into two hungry crows who came flying down to get me.

X

Lulú   Amancio.

Amancio *comes back from his trance-like state and looks at* **Lulú** *again.*

Lulú   I'm not sure you've noticed, but the ground is covered with apples that have fallen from the trees. There are so many it's impossible to see the ground.

Calisto *and* **Abelardo** *enter.*

Calisto   I've been telling him for the last few days, but I'm not sure what's going on. I don't know if he just doesn't hear me, or he just doesn't care about what I'm saying.

Abelardo   I have too many things going on, and I can't do it all. That's it.

Calisto *turns around to talk to his father.*

Calisto   I only know that we're several weeks behind schedule, and if we don't hurry up, we'll lose this year's harvest.

Amancio   Are you telling me you still haven't conducted the apple-ripening test?

Abelardo   Let me repeat: I've got tons of things to deal with, and I can't do it all. Do I need to tattoo it on my face, or how the hell do you need me to tell you?

Calisto I have no clue, but the labourers are idling while waiting for our instructions, don't you think?

Abelardo They might be idling because they haven't been paid for weeks, not because I might or might not have done the ripening test. Don't you think that might be the reason they've started protesting?

Amancio Is that true, Calisto?

Calisto What?

Amancio You still haven't paid the labourers?

Calisto and **Abelardo** *look at the floor.*

Calisto I apologize. I've never had any problem with my duties, but lately –

Abelardo Lately, we don't know what's going on with us.

Lulú I'm not sure you can listen to me, but there's something I'd like to tell you.

They all look at her.

You've been very good to me, and I've been very happy by your side, but the time has come for me to say goodbye. I'm leaving.

Calisto and **Abelardo** *look at their father, surprised by* **Lulú**'s *words.*

Amancio What are you talking about, Lulú? We're crazy about you, and we cherish you!

Calisto Absolutely! What bullshit is this?

Abelardo You're kidding, right?

There is no answer.

Amancio Lulú, please, look at me. Since you moved in, we're the happiest men on the face of the Earth. I have no clue what's going on in your mind, but if you think we don't love you enough, that you're bothering us or anything like that, let me tell you that you're completely mistaken. Don't you realize how important you are to us? That we would do anything for you if you only asked?

He stops talking to **Lulú**, *looks at* **Abelardo** *and starts talking to him.*

Amancio For example, you, Abelardo. Of all your possessions, which do you value most?

Abelardo   Me? Why?

Amancio   Of everything that you own. Tell Lulú.

Abelardo   Huh?

Amancio   Answer! What's your most prized possession?

Abelardo *thinks about it.*

Abelardo   My shotgun.

Amancio   What about you, Calisto?

Calisto   Out of everything I own?

Amancio   Yes.

Calisto   My motorbike. It's what I love most.

Amancio   Did you hear that? The shotgun, the motorbike and, for me, my apple orchard. Those are the three things that we cherish the most. Now listen to me. Should we have to prove our love, Lulú, I'm certain that, right now, Calisto would throw his motorbike over a cliff; Abelardo would break his shotgun in a thousand pieces; and I would set the farm on fire. If we had to show you how we really feel about you – we would do anything for you.

Lulú   Anything?

Amancio   Absolutely anything.

Lulú *thinks about it.*

Lulú   Come here and give me a hug.

Calisto, **Abelardo** *and* **Amancio** *get close to* **Lulú**, *and the four of them embrace tightly.*

Amancio   And now, promise that you will never leave our side and that we will all be very happy together.

Calisto   Very happy together.

Pause.

Abelardo   Very happy together.

XI

Amancio   It's difficult for me to explain what happened next. First, because the guilt, the shame and the disgust forbid me to. And then because what we did could be called the greatest aberration that a father could carry out with his sons. Something that animals would never do. A horrible perversion that not even the sickest mind would ever come up with. Right after it took place, we went to our rooms, and we did not wake up until the moon came up and then down – the following day.

Pause.

We got up and left our rooms as if nothing had happened; we took our places at the table as we did the night before. No breakfast, no lunch or snacks, just dinner, and for dessert, Lulú again. Our heads could hold thoughts only about Lulú; there was space only for Lulú – Lulú and only Lulú. Until one night, in the middle of our recklessness – a bitter wind started whistling, windows blew wide open and everything started to fill with smoke, smoke that came from the orchard and forced me to bolt.

Pause.

When I arrived and stopped at the apple trees, there were no more flames. The fire was extinguished, and all the trees had turned to ashes. Trees, Calisto's motorbike and, on top of it, Abelardo's shotgun.

Pause.

How could such a thing happen? What happened?

Pause.

I don't know, but as soon as I turned around to look at my sons –

He looks at **Calisto** *and* **Abelardo**. *They are next to their father, sad, with a lost gaze*

– they were white as ghosts, their bodies were covered with wounds and they could hardly speak.

XII

Julián   Are you still doing it?

Amancio   What?

Julián   I'm asking you if you're still doing it.

Amancio   Well, we tried, but we don't know what's wrong with us.

Julián   What do you mean?

Amancio   That every time she looks at us, something takes us over, and we can't help it.

Julián   So, are you still doing it?

He looks at the three men. No one answers him.

Amancio   You're going to think I am crazy, but last night, I couldn't help myself – I don't know how I got the strength, but – I took the axe to her neck. I dragged her down the stairs, and I locked her up in the basement.

Julián *stays silent.*

Amancio   I know full well that it was the wrong way to fix things, but we had tried so many times before. My sons are getting worse every day, and – I don't know – we don't know what to do. We're desperate.

Julián   Here, have a drink. It will do you good.

Amancio *takes the glass that* **Julián** *offers him and downs it all at once.*

Amancio   Julián, be honest. What do you think is happening to us? I keep thinking about it, and I can't get to the bottom of it.

Julián *looks again at* **Amancio**, *who is still with his two sick sons.*

Julián   It's still too early to know exactly what's going on, and I don't want to take a wild guess, but – a story came to mind while you were telling me yours, and who knows? It might help you.

He starts looking for something.

But before I tell you about it, I'd like to read you something very few people know. And I'm sure it will help you to understand what I'm trying to explain much better.

Amancio   Tell me that you believe everything we're telling you. Or do you think we've all gone mad?

Julián   Let's not rush to conclusions.

He finds what he was looking for: a book.

For the time being, listen very carefully and pay attention.

He opens the book and starts reading.

'The Book of Genesis. Chapter 1. In the beginning, when God created the heavens and the Earth, the Earth was a formless void, and darkness covered the face of the deep, while a wind from God swept over –' Wait,

I'll skip this part and jump to the ending. Verse 26. Listen: 'Then God said, "Let us make humankind in our image, according to our likeness; and let them have dominion over the fish of the sea, and over the birds of the air, and over the cattle, and over all the wild animals of the Earth, and over every creeping thing that creeps upon the Earth". So God created humankind in his image, in the image of God he created them; male and female he created them.' Now, here, Chapter 2, Verse 21: 'Then the LORD God said, "It is not good that the man should be alone". So the LORD God caused a deep sleep to fall upon the man, and he slept; then he took one of his ribs and closed up its place with flesh. And the rib that the LORD God had taken from the man he made into a woman and brought her to the man. Then the man said, "This at last is bone of my bones and flesh of my flesh; this one shall be called Woman, for out of Man this one was taken".'

He looks up and at the three men again.

Did you notice something strange?

Amancio   What?

Julián   Something strange, something that caught your attention.

Amancio   Why are you asking us this?

Julián   Because of the story.

Amancio   I have no clue what you mean.

Julián   Did you notice something that doesn't make sense?

Amancio *looks at his sons for answers, but neither* **Abelardo** *nor* **Calisto** *says anything.*

Amancio   Like what?

Julián   A hole.

Amancio   A what?

Julián   Or a jump.

Amancio   I have no clue.

Julián   I'm asking you if you see anything strange between the first and second chapters, something that didn't fit.

There's no answer.

Look, in the first chapter of Genesis, it says that God created humankind in his image; he created male and female, right?

Amancio   Yes, that's what it says.

Julián   And then in the second chapter, we're told that Adam felt alone, and feeling alone wasn't good, so God took one of Adam's ribs, and the rib that the LORD God had taken from the man he made into a woman.

Amancio   Yes, so what?

Julián   Well, if God had already created woman in his image and out of clay at the same time he created Adam, how come now, in the second chapter, the Bible says that Adam felt alone, and God has to create another woman from Adam's rib?

There's no answer.

What happened to the first woman?

There's no answer.

The other one, the woman God created in his likeness, not the one created with Adam's rib – whatever happened to her?

Amancio *looks at his sons again; they still do not say anything.*

Julián   And why in the second chapter, after God created the woman out of Adam's rib, does Adam say, 'This one at last is bone of my bones and flesh of my flesh'? This one? What does *this one* mean? It means that the previous one, the one God created out of clay, was not bone of his bones and flesh of his flesh. Why does he make a point of saying 'this one'?

Amancio, **Calisto** *and* **Abelardo** *stay silent.*

Julián   Don't fret. Even though it's been read for thousands of years, almost everybody skims over this part, and only a few notice it. Actually, most priests die without having noticed it.

He reaches for something.

Forgive me, but I'm looking for something that I want you all to see.

He puts the Bible down and takes another book.

Oh, yes, here it is.

He opens the book and looks for a page. He shows it to **Amancio** *and his two sons.*

Julián   Look carefully. Do you know what it is?

The three men look at each other.

Amancio   A painting?

Julián   Yes, but what else?

The three men look at each other again.

Abelardo   A painting.

Julián   What does it portray?

Calisto   Adam and Eve, or so it seems.

Julián   Yes, it's *The Fall of Man and Expulsion from the Garden of Eden* to be exact, a fresco that Michelangelo painted in the Sistine Chapel.

He points to the inside of the book.

And who is he?

Amancio *and his two sons look inside the book again.*

Amancio   Adam?

Julián *points to another section in the book.*

Julián   And this woman right here?

The three men keep looking inside the book.

Amancio   Eve.

Julián   Perfect, but if he's Adam, and she's Eve . . .

He points to a third section inside the book.

This woman, up here, all wrapped up in the tree trunk, who do you think she is?

There's no answer.

This one – she looks like a woman from the waist up, but from the waist down, she has the body of a reptile.

Neither **Amancio** *nor his sons say anything.*

Julián   Do you remember the passages I just read to you? About God creating a woman out of the man's rib, but he had already created another one out of clay at the same that he created Adam?

There's no answer.

Well, that's her. And here she is – L, I, L, I, T, H – Lilith. She's the woman that God created out of clay and that, by the second chapter, has vanished and we never hear about her – Adam's first wife – ever again. Do you know why they removed her from the Bible? Why did they take her out of the Creation story, and why did they leave Eve's episode?

Amancio *does not answer.*

Julián   Because when Adam possessed her for the very first time, Lilith wanted to be on top, in the position Adam had claimed, and he refused. He told her no and then forced her to be under him for the whole act. Once they finished, they had an argument. Since both had been created in God's image and were equal, Lilith could not understand why Adam could subject her by being on top of her, while she was denied the same opportunity.

Pause.

Realizing that Adam was not going to change his mind, Lilith complained to God. God told her that he understood her, but nevertheless, she was to obey Adam. And do you know what Lilith did then?

The three men shake their heads.

Amancio   No.

Julián   Full of anger, she left Eden on her own, and God punished her and condemned her to wander for all eternity and made her the first vampire in history.

He shuts the book.

Do you remember the goatherd? The one who was your father's friend and died a long time ago?

Amancio *looks at* **Julián** *and his two sons, waiting for an answer.*

Amancio   Do you mean Benancio?

Julián   Exactly. Do you know what happened?

There's no answer.

What actually happened?

There's no answer.

A woman also crossed his path, and soon thereafter, he found all his herd dead, and his only son had drowned in the ocean.

Pause.

Do you remember how he died? How they found him?

Amancio   He was hanging from a barn beam.

Julián   Yes, upside down, like a pig, and with a bite on the back of his neck.

He goes behind the young men and looks at their necks.

The goatherd was the first person to tell me a story similar to what you just told me. And let me tell you, it's not the first time, not even the second, that someone has come to me with your kind of story: men who meet a beautiful woman and, bit by bit, without realizing it, with sex and lust, they have been left ruined and doomed.

Amancio   Julián, be clear, what do you mean?

Julián   I'm just sharing all this information with you because you and your sons might not be to blame for what's happening around you. More than likely, from Adam's first wife to the goatheard's woman to that Lulú, they might not be that different – actually, they're all the same.

Pause.

You did the right thing by calling only me. Doctors and police don't care about matters that transcend physical and concrete reality. Matters of the soul often escape them. And in spiritual matters, there is also plenty of misery, constriction and rotting. There's so much rot that the souls of many people end up a dumping ground, full of dangerous diseases, and the greatest of all, Amancio, is suffering from the devil: a tainted vermin, who, contrary to what most people believe, is not male, but female. A woman, still resentful, because she cannot accept that her Creator put man in control of the entire planet and everything on it, including her. What many women still do not understand is that women were created to be the property of men and not the other way around. Almighty God willed it that way, so commanded it, and believing otherwise would be against His word. You only have to read the oldest book in history to realize that I'm telling you the only truth. Truth as real as you having that woman locked in your basement and us having this conversation right here right now.

Pause.

Evil exists, Amancio, it is alive, and its presence in the world we live in is increasingly palpable. Why does it choose some people and not others? We don't know, but what I can tell you is that Satan observes us, analyses our weaknesses, and that's often where he entraps us. The devil is here, and it's far from a fairy tale. The devil is a woman thirsty for revenge who, whenever she has the opportunity, leaves the underworld with the mission to drive men crazy and kill their children. She already did it. The first time, going back to Eden, disguised as a snake and through the apple, and she continues to this day. Look at all the ways she tempted your children and you; all this time, seducing you and toying with your weak flesh.

Amancio, *still listening intensely, does not say anything.*

Julián   Amancio, God created both heaven and Earth and everything in between without any problem. But when it was time to create woman, he erred. Man was easy, but with woman, He made a mistake and had to repeat the experiment. That's why they had to remove the episode of Lilith from the Holy Scriptures – because God was wrong, and to hide His failure, He had to hide her, too.

He walks towards **Amancio** *and stops inches away from him, grabs him by the shoulders, and stares at him.*

Julián   Has it ever occurred to you that Lulú, who appeared in front of you, under that apple tree, could actually be that same snake that killed your wife and you wasted so much time going after?

There's no answer.

You told me that, one day, you hit the snake with an axe, and you almost cut her in half. Isn't that right?

There's no answer.

And doesn't it seem strange that she appeared in front of you with the wound on her back that, the following day, had mysteriously healed?

Pause.

Amancio   Yes – very quickly.

Julián   What about those stockings that you say she always wears? Why do you think she never takes them off?

There's no answer.

Julián   Come on, you three, answer me. Why do you think she never takes them off?

Abelardo   According to her, when she was a young girl, she spilled a pot of boiling oil on herself and burned them.

Julián   Sure! And you three believed it. Did it ever occur to you that she could be hiding something else under those stockings? Don't you remember what she told you about Lulú not being a real name but a nickname shared by all names that start with 'Lu'? Amancio, the double effort that God had to do is the reason there is only one seed from man, but there are two seeds for woman: the seed from Eve and the seed from –?

There's no answer.

The seed from Lu – Do you get it, Amancio?

There's no answer.

The seed from Lu –

Silence.

Amancio   The seed from Lucifer.

XIII

*A **Woman** appears. She greatly resembles **Lulú**, yet she looks and acts differently.*

Woman   I don't believe that they would erase Lilith's episode just to hide the fact that God was not perfect because He made a mistake. However, I do think that they had an ulterior motive. There are two sides to every story, two sides of the same coin. It happened to Lilith, it happened to me and it also happened to Amancio's wife. It is plausible that, contrary to the story Amancio shares, she did not die from any snakebite. One night, tired of being belittled and treated like crap, she fled her home like Lilith left Eden. Her family decided to kill her off and erase every trace of her rather than assume responsibility for what had actually happened. That explains why every Sunday, they would visit the tomb they made for her and leave candles. Probably no woman is buried there. Just dirt on top of dirt and underneath that dirt, an empty coffin. Constantly repeat a lie, and falsehoods slowly but surely take on the appearance of the truth. The secret lies in creating a parallel explanation that hides everything we want concealed. Then we allow fallacies to take root until they become the only versions of the truth. It wasn't true that Amancio knew nothing about me when he found me injured beneath that apple tree. Quite the contrary. Even though, for him, all women were practically the same, and he usually couldn't differentiate us, he had seen me around plenty of times. Lucía Liébanas Hernández: a day labourer, who, having spent many years working on the farm, suffered an unfortunate accident. One afternoon, while I was pruning a tree, a branch fell on top of me. I fell to the ground and, when I woke up –

Amancio Calisto *and* **Abelardo**, *carrying pick axes and shovels, appear and stand behind the* **Woman**.

Woman   – when I woke up, I found myself inside the house, dizzy, not knowing how I got there.

Amancio   This is what we usually do with the labourers who have an accident or get sick.

Calisto   We provide you with bedrest –

Abelardo   – we feed you every day –

Amancio   – and we take care of you until you're healthy again.

Woman   They took care of me until my wound healed. But as soon as I recovered and thanked them for all their care, I told them that I wanted to return to the mill, and they didn't like that.

Amancio   We give them our best –

Abelardo   – we put a lot of effort into it, and in the end –

Calisto   – in the end, they all end up treating us the same way as before. Always.

Amancio   I'm not sure how they manage, but they always take advantage of our good will.

Abelardo   It's always the same story, but we never learn.

Calisto   I can't believe we've been fooled yet again. Unbelievable.

Amancio   They must think we're idiots or something.

Abelardo   Or maybe we are really idiots.

Calisto   Why are women so ungrateful?

Amancio   I don't know, but, first, she should repent for what she's done to us.

Abelardo   Yes, and then apologize to us –

Calisto   And then she should return all the money she cost us.

Woman   Then they took me to the kitchen, pushed me inside and kicked me to the ground.

Abelardo   From now on, you'll sleep next to the oven.

Calisto   The kitchen will be your room.

Amancio   And your name will no longer be Lucía. From now on, you are Lulú.

Woman   And that's how they went from taking care of me to locking me up and humiliating me whenever they could. One evening, after I cooked them dinner, they asked me to take off my clothes and dance naked for them. But I refused, and both father and sons reacted worse than ever.

Amancio   You put a dagger through our hearts as passionately as you caressed them early on. And now you are not leaving unscathed.

Calisto   You can't.

Abelardo   It wouldn't be fair.

Woman   And as soon as they stopped talking, they dragged me to the basement, threw me on a mattress, and, pointing the shotgun at me, unleashed on me the cruellest acts a person's body can bear. Violent people always need someone to blame for all the misfortunes that happen to them. They need to destroy others in order to feel superior and claim their place in the world; that's how the hearts of those who keep deceiving themselves work. They are enemies of the truth. They have chosen to live in the shadows and rot in the dark night instead of living in the light. That's why they fenced the house with barbed wire and locked me in the basement. If you're going to do something you don't want anyone to find out about, you better do it in a place where no one sees you. I don't remember how long exactly I was down in the basement. They barely brought me water to drink, fed me only once a day, and each day turned into an endless appointment with horror. Until one afternoon, the door screeched and behind the door –

Julián *enters and stands next to the group of men.*

Woman   – Amancio appeared with that man. A man I had never met and who carried in one hand an axe and in the other a crucifix. They silently came down the stairs, approached the old mattress where I was lying and, without letting go of the axe or the cross, that man turned to me and said –

Julián   I'm not sure if you realize the damage you've inflicted on this family, but you've done a hell of a job.

Woman   And, right away, Amancio grabbed me violently, tore my stockings apart, and upon seeing the burns on my feet, the man with the crucifix raised his axe towards the sky and while shouting –

Julián   It's her!

Woman   – struck my legs with his axe.

Pause.

They could have struck me again to finish me off all at once, so I would not have suffered for so long. But, no, they did not. Instead, they just stood there, watching me crawl on the floor while I bled to death.

Julián   This time, Lulú, you're not getting away with it.

Woman   Those were the last words I heard while still alive. And with the scant strength left in someone about to die, the last thing that came out of my lips was 'My name is not Lulú'.

Pause.

'My name is Lucía.'

Pause.

Whether he believed it or not, there was never any type of romance or consensual relationship between Amancio and me. Never. What actually happened differs greatly from his version. As it was tirelessly explained to me, the problem is that a woman can't show gratitude or affection towards a group of men without them thinking she's a whore. Because that's what they called me, me and every other female labourer working on the property. They also told us that we were atrocities of nature, seen once in a lifetime but can never be forgotten – women who drag men to the edge of a cliff and wait for them to take one step further and fall off. And finally, for each lie, there's an apple tree, and for each apple tree, there's another woman who has lost her life. That's how this story ends. There are no vampires or demons. There is a forest that's exhausted from witnessing all these atrocities, of hearing all these lies, and one night decides to set itself on fire so that it may catch or chase after all those malicious men. It's a desperate cry for help from an Earth that aches so much it begins to show its pain in the form of fire. A cloud of ashes lingers, a reminder to us all that ever since the world began, there have always been two stories. One we know about and one that is hidden. What we call our reality, what surrounds us, always revolves around something that we are constantly told or were told a long time ago. Our world, where we live and die, rotates on the axes that stories build. That's why for life to mean something, we should all have the opportunity to explain who we really were and what happened to us. Being able to come back, from wherever we may be, and finally tell the story – the other side of the story.

The **Woman** *lies down with her back on the floor, closes her eyes, and the three men –* **Amancio,** **Calisto** *and* **Abelardo,** *carrying shovels and pick axes – surround her.* **Julián** *grabs a cross and points it towards the sky.*

I Die for I Die Not

The Double Life of Teresa

A woman, between fifteen and sixty-six years old, addresses an audience filled with people of different genders and ages.

The Longest Night in History

I departed life on Earth on what is known as 'the longest night in history'. Time had to be aligned between men and the stars once and for all, and, coincidence or not, the day I died was chosen for the calendar update. Until then, days were organized according to the Julian calendar, but that night, the Gregorian calendar, which we still use, was introduced. Due to the many details that had to be ironed out, the ten days following my death are nowhere to be found; they just vanished with the stroke of a pen. Similarly, my body vanished the moment it relinquished life. My heart stayed in the same place where it stopped beating, in Alba de Tormes, but the rest of my body quickly dispersed throughout the planet.

The Infinite Body

Let me explain it to you. Shortly after my blood stopped flowing through my veins, this foot had already reached Rome; this piece of jaw, Italy; all these teeth back here, Mexico; this piece of collarbone, Belgium; the fingers on this hand, except for the thumb and the pinky, Brussels, Seville and Paris; and the right hand, Portugal. However, before its arrival in Portugal, my hand toured the United States of America with two Discalced Carmelite nuns. Upon their arrival at customs, the nuns realized they had to declare the hand. Unfortunately, there was no box to check for 'incorrupt members', but then one of the nuns had the astute idea to declare it under 'canned and pickled goods'.

The rest of my body remained in Ávila. All but my right eye and this hand right here; as soon as they chopped it off, they put it in an envelope and, as if it were a piece of ham, shipped it to Lisbon. From Lisbon to Coímbra, from Coímbra to Valladolid, from Valladolid to Burgos – it just kept getting out and about until it finally landed in Ronda, where it has remained these last years. I am saying *where it remained* because, not too long ago, I jumped over the walls of the Church of the Merced and took it back. The last part of my body that I needed to recapture: my left hand. I swear there are days when I look at myself in the mirror, and I still cannot believe it.

You cannot imagine how gruelling it has been for me to get here. As a matter of fact, if I told you everything I endured to restore myself, I am positive you would think me a liar or a fool, one or the other. And it would not surprise me at all. Do you want to know why? Because my story, the story I am here to tell you, is not one of your run-of-the-mill stories.

First Life

I am Teresa. I am the third of ten siblings, and I always treasured literature, so much so that, as a little girl, I would never be found without a book in my hands. My favourite genres were the lives of the saints and chivalry novels. One day, a series of titles intended exclusively for the religious elite were translated into our vulgar language, and my father brought them all home. Little did he know that, overnight, the Church would issue the *List of Prohibited Books* (*Index Librorum Prohibitorum*), and I would be forced to quit my newly found pleasure. The Authorities were clear: Whoever is found in possession of any of the indexed titles shall be executed. But I just didn't care and, instead of obeying the decree, I refused to incinerate the words nourishing my soul. Why should I have to throw my books into the fire? But the day my mother died, right after we came back from burying her, I realized that all my bookshelves had been emptied. Two of my most cherished possessions, my mother and my books, vanished on the same day. Sadness overwhelmed me. So much that there was not even one evening when I did not go to bed crying or a morning when I did not wake up agonized with pain. But, after a while, I met a young man who courted me, and I started talking to him.

A Nun? Not on Your Life

The young man was nice enough, and we enjoyed each other's company, but I was not like other girls and getting married was completely out of the question. One day my father asked me about the young man, and my answer was crystal clear: 'I'd rather die than marry a man!' My poor father, appalled upon hearing those words, confined me in the Agustinas Convent right away.

At the Agustinas – basically, they taught you only how to sew and how to wait. But marriage was still not for me, so I pretended to sew, and I was definitely not waiting for anyone. I was no longer a child. I had relished life's pleasures, and I just wanted to put on beautiful dresses and go out and dance. Anything but be a nun. A nun? Not on your life.

But at one point, I was forced to choose, so into the convent I went. Against my father's wishes, I still chose the convent. And I chose it, not because I heard God's call, but rather because, after getting married, women are forced to be submissive and compliant, and I find that degrading and unacceptable. Just look at how men drain, not only their wives' lives, but also their soul right after they get married. That's why, one morning at dawn, without being noticed, I flee to the Encarnación Convent. And it is there, right after I put on my robe, a strange illness strikes me, and I am immobilized in a bed for more than three years.

Arsenal of Diseases

I felt as if I were lying on a bed of hot coals. My nerves were on fire. I shake incessantly and scream out loud. My father was right: my health deteriorated quickly just because I did not want to marry a man. For two years, I could not eat or drink without help, and I suffered so many illnesses I turned into an arsenal of diseases. One afternoon – I was just flesh and bones – they took my pulse and declared me dead. I had stopped breathing. And right away, they close my eyes and start digging my grave.

Interior Garden

But one of the candles that lights up the bedroom accidentally sets the sheets on fire. Smoke penetrates my nose, and, all of a sudden, I regain consciousness. My throat is dry; my eyes are full of wax, and my tongue is lacerated because I had been biting it. Nobody understands what might have happened to me, but the first words out of my mouth say I want to return to the Encarnación Convent. Once again, my father tries to convince me to marry that young man, but, again, I refuse. And I do not give up until I am finally within the convent walls. For the next three years, I will lie on a bed in the infirmary. Three very long years. Fortunately, an uncle of mine gave me a book he had managed to save from the burning and saved my life in the process. Thanks to all those words that filled me so deeply, I managed to get out of bed one afternoon and resume my life inside the convent. But when I get to my bedroom, more than a cell, what I find is a luxury apartment: two separate rooms with beautiful views overlooking an interior garden.

Lifestyle and Customs

The convent is packed with the daughters of the most important aristocratic houses of Castile. At first, it does not bother me, but as the days go by, I pay attention to the lifestyle they lead inside and outside the order. I didn't know it then, but the convent nuns can still see people from outside; they are even allowed to spend a night outside and return the next day. It creates an ordeal I have to suffer, since the young man whom I left so as not to have to marry learns of my whereabouts and starts visiting me. I am not amused, and I complain to the Mother Superior, but she forces me to engage in conversations with him. 'We need money, and you have to do it for the sake of the monastery,' she tells me. So as soon as I return to my beautiful garden apartment, I undress from head to toe, lie face down on the floor and close my eyes tightly until I have a –

First Revelation

A place for recollection, where all goods are shared, and social status is irrelevant. A place where religious seclusion is observed, and riches are despised. A humble convent devoted to praying. Not a refectory nor an inn. A place for meditation, contemplative life and work, a lot of work. A place for prayers and perseverance. Not just a temple but a beacon that shines light upon the rest of the world. Yes, Teresa, you must walk towards the edge of the precipice. You must stop at the edge of the cliff, and then you must jump. Jump without any fear, for fear is the devil, and your only obligation is to reform the Order. You shall carry it out even though many will feel threatened and deem you a danger. But you shall accomplish your mission: you shall be known as Teresa de Jesús, and you shall rescind all privileges from those you consider unworthy.

Public Enemy

I no sooner set foot back at Encarnación Convent than I learn that all the nuns are barricading themselves in their rooms and calling for my arrest. They know full well that my plan is to return them to austerity, and they are all against changing their lives. And not only the nuns are against me – the whole Order mistrusts me and finds me highly suspicious. Because for all my incessant talk of the merits of personal prayer, I waste my time in dreary conversations. Because I foist the vote of obedience on everybody, but I cannot let anyone tell me what to do. And because I claim to have a vocation, but, truth be told, becoming a nun was the only way to avoid getting married to a man.

Teresa against the Inquisition

And yes, maybe they are right when they say that the convent was invented as the only way to escape the claws of man, but for the life of me, I cannot comprehend why, even after becoming nuns, we are still restrained by men's shackles. Why must our lives still be controlled by male desires? Where is it written? And since we are talking about writing – yes, I know, I realize that it was bold of me to write a book since I know full well that women are not allowed to be cultured, but my confessor asked me to do it. And you know very well that I am not one to be contrarian.

However, if you ask me how God appears to me, I really cannot help you. All I can tell you is that it is like an overwhelming bright light, pure, and it is all light, a soft and blurry clarity, a brightness that delights your eyesight and fills you with immense pleasure. I do not know how to explain it accurately, but it is the complete opposite of watching the murky, muddy water that flows on Earth. Rather, the light is very much alive, far from dead, like lightning bursting in the middle of the night. So majestic and impressive a light that anyone who encounters it will be certain of its source. Every time God abandons me, no matter how desperately I want to see Him again, I am unable to invoke him. Because if I could, then it would be an imaginary and not a true presence.

That is what my book is about. I analyse my experiences; I write them down and corroborate them. Some people think it is an autobiography, while for others, it is an invitation to religious seclusion and personal prayer. But I believe that, overall, it is more of a manual, a guide about how anyone, man or woman, can achieve a state of maximum autonomy that is nothing but the capacity to think by yourself without being shepherded by anyone else.

But you, Inquisitors, you have never feared the physical strength of the populace that you manipulate. What you actually fear is that the people can expand and develop their intelligence. That is why I have reformed the Carmelo Order, thus dividing the Church because I truly believe that thinking is not only for men. If any woman wants to weave and sew, let her do it because sewing is not a sin, but she should also know that life is more than just yarns and threads; she should know that, above all, life is to ponder and to question. And do you know why? Because inside each and every human being stands a castle built of diamonds, a fortress with many quarters and a main room. Precisely in that room, all our questions are answered. Our hands, our eyes and everything that shapes us are mere traps, deceits that humour us but distract us from what is essential. That is the reason my nuns and I flee this Earth and everything that prevents us from asking: Who truly lives inside us? And we pray for the answer. But not any prayer will do. It cannot be vocal or the kind you declaim out loud; only internal prayers will do. Those who do not realize who they are praying to, those who do not even know what they are praying for or how they are doing it; those who mumble whatever they come up with and just move their lips and waste saliva, those people are not praying, they are not even close. To me, repetition for repetition's sake is not praying.

And that's where you have the problem. You, Inquisitors, have always feared that people might get to know themselves, let alone that they might question who they are and what their purpose is on this Earth. You only care about the populace following your strict rules, following whatever law you write, and, most important, not stepping out of your prescribed bounds. A society that can think for itself does not need anyone's superior guidance to draw its own conclusions. That is what terrifies you, Inquisitors. If people like me have succeeded, on our own, in posing questions about God's meaning, why couldn't we then pose questions about our own life? There have been many ways of directing society's will but none more popular than moulding their thoughts – that and always denigrating their capacity to conjure up other realities. And limiting people's dreams, that has been your Church's pride and glory. If it were not so, why would you be so afraid of a bunch of women? Please, Inquisitors, do tell me, what do you think my nuns and I might be doing while locked up in a convent? I know I am not being accused for writing a book, for having Jewish ancestry, nor for being enlightened. I am actually being accused for having dared to teach people what the word *freedom* means. You, Inquisitors, have only understood one thing: that keeping people truly poor has nothing to do with money. Spiritual starvation – that is what being poor really means. Being poor does not involve finances but souls. And nothing works more efficiently than limiting their knowledge. That is why you are obsessed with punishing anyone who dares to get near a book.

The Holy Office

The Holy Inquisition was an organization that essentially required you to suspect your neighbour. Any accusation, whether true or false, anonymous or not, was welcome. And every time an accusation was filed, a new case was opened, and the inquisitors would begin investigating the person. You can all imagine the outcome. The rumour mill running amok and public trials in every city and town. Actually, it is not all that different from what you have on TV nowadays. I am talking about all those shows rife with journalists who believe they are judges, and people defending themselves from libels and slanders. That is why Spaniards are always afraid to stand out. Think about it. Why are we so afraid to be centre stage? Why are we so afraid of personal growth? In this country, you can triumph, but we all know that every Spaniard has the right tools to bring anyone down. That is why, in Spain, if you show off your talent, you are close to committing suicide. Instead of envying the outstanding, Spaniards look down on them and not because of the light they emanate but just because they dare to be different, knowing full well that millions are ready to take them down.

Answered Prayers

But the Inquisition does not condemn me – it lets me go. Still, they sure keep me under close surveillance all the time because they know that people are talking incessantly about me, and my mere presence can easily irritate everyone around me. But I couldn't care less and keep doing my own thing, which is to establish convents, so I can protect my women from men. From Ávila to Medina del Campo, from Medina del Campo to Malagón, from Malagón to Valladolid, from Valladolid to Toledo, from Toledo to Pastrana, from Pastrana to Salamanca, from Salamanca to Alba de Tormes, from Alba de Tormes to Segovia and from Segovia to Beas del Segura, where I suddenly realize I am no longer a young woman. I have turned sixty and can no longer do it all on my own. I've fallen sick again. And right there and then, I have the great good fortune to meet Father Gracián; a well-travelled man and a Discalced Carmelite. He was exactly what I had been searching for all that time. Finally, my prayers had been answered, and I couldn't be any happier. But my happiness is short-lived since, right after meeting Father Gracián, I am prohibited from writing, from establishing convents; they even prohibit me from going outside. I have become a *persona non grata* and, thus, I am not welcomed anywhere. They say I have started a war, and they are not completely wrong, to tell you the truth.

The River of My Life

I shall remain in Ávila for the next four years. I am ill and facing the Tormes River. Its waters witnessed my birth and, soon enough, will witness my death. But that is not the worst part. The worst part is that when I needed Father Gracián the most, he stopped answering my letters and just vanished into thin air. I never find out why because shortly after I send him my last letter, I am stricken by a very high fever, and I immediately die.

End of the First Part

You already know what comes next; I told you right at the beginning. Right after I die, Father Gracián, who not even once came to visit while I was sick, showed up in front of my cadaver and turned my funeral into a slaughter. He hung me on a hook upside down and started to chop at me with a saw, as if I were a hog. Then he divided me up and put me in different packages that he shipped all over the globe. You also know the places where my body ended up. You know everything except for one thing: how, five hundred years later, did I return to this world?

Second Life

The day that I landed on Earth again, I knew only two things: I was alone and lost. Until one afternoon, completely by chance, I walked in front of a mirror and realized that, apart from being lost and alone, I was insubstantial – you might say I was nothing but air. And you have to understand that, unlike the resurrected Christ, I did not have a body handy in which to reincarnate. I had only terror and way too many questions. Who was the real me? Where was my body? And why couldn't I remember anything at all? I kept asking myself all these questions until one night, surprisingly, an army of words invaded me.

My Cadaver

Oh, how long is this life! How hard these wanderings, this cell, and these irons in which this soul is held! What was that, and where did those sentences come from? 'I have no clue,' I thought. I quickly forgot about it and started doing some other tasks until, a few days later, it happened again. Another group of words, different from before, crept up on me. *I live without living in me, and such is my hope, that I die, for I die not.* This went on and on for weeks. But, one day, among all those words, a name finally appeared: *Teresa de Jesús.* Right there and then, from my innermost conscience, memories started sprouting in my head: the Encarnación Convent, my good old father, the young man who courted me, the Holy Church, my long illness – the first question had been answered. At last, I knew who I was and where I came from. Now it was time for me to find out what was I doing on Earth for the second time and where I could find my body.

I thought I should start frequenting libraries to start my enquiry. I could never imagine what all those rivers of ink were about to tell me. Rome, Toledo, Antwerp, Ghent, Sevilla, Valladolid, Mexico, Málaga, Lisbon, Paris, Sanlúcar de Barrameda – how was it possible to be in so many places at once? I kept on searching until I found the answer: my cadaver was not just a cadaver; it was the cadaver of a saint, which meant that every inch of my body was a relic. Do you know approximately how much one of my ribs would cost you? How much would you pay for my right eye or this finger right here? Incalculable. It has no price. And if it had a price, it would be so mind-boggling that nobody could ever pay it. And rightfully so. After all, look at me. Who would have guessed I'd look this good after having been carved up five centuries ago? I don't look a day over five hundred years, don't you agree?

In Search of the Lost Body

Let me assure you that I am not bonkers and that everything I am telling you is absolutely true, even though I cannot prove it. Every time I recovered one of my body parts, I would replace it with an exact replica, so the alarm would not go off. This way, I could get each and every one of my nails back safely before I got my nose, for example, and why nobody suspects my desecrations, as if desecrating yourself were even possible. But what was I supposed to do once I recovered my arms, my legs, my teeth and lips, my heart? Where should I go, and what was my path? And while I was pondering, all of a sudden, I heard a noise, and I felt a luminous presence on my back.

A Sign

He might have been around fifty years old. Upon seeing me, walking all alone by the side of the road, he kindly stopped and invited me to climb onto his truck. He was from the south; he was transporting produce and driving back home. While driving, he talked to me about his job, his dog and his wife, in that order, and his words were anything but kind. He complained all the time, mostly about the poor decisions he had made throughout his life. I was exhausted; I only wanted to sleep, and my silence did not seem to bother him. In fact, he never once asked me to speak.

When we got close to Madrid, he took a knife out of his pocket and put it to my throat.

First Steps

Barefoot and completely disoriented, I stopped at the entrance of a building that, given its state, seemed abandoned. I looked for a corner and fell asleep. When I woke, my body was covered in bruises. and my crotch was bleeding. I observed the way my blood ran down my leg, and first I thought of God and then about what had happened the night before inside that truck. 'What good did it do me to get my body back?' I asked myself. Right away, my stomach growled. 'How many centuries since I last ate?' Then I left the building and started walking around until I spotted a sort of garbage container. It was not huge, but it was surrounded by a group of cats that would not stop meowing. I got close to them; I raised the lid, and together, we devoured everything that was inside – like beasts.

Garbage

Trashed food is not too awful. Sometimes, depending on how long since it was thrown away, it can have a bitter taste. But like everything in this life, you have to know where to go to find what you need. Not all garbage is created equal. This trashcan here is not like that one over there. Likewise, a central subway stop is very different from one in a poor neighbourhood. And that is why I decide to settle down in Plaza Mayor, Madrid's main square. My first days are rough, but I meet other homeless people, people who have been homeless for a very long time, and with their help, I learn to manoeuvre the world of mendicancy.

Until one day, I meet a young man who sleeps two arches away to my right, and we become friends. At sunset, we gather all our money and go to the supermarket to do our shopping, which is nothing more than two cans of sardines and several boxes of wine. Truth be told, in order to become a bona fide beggar, you need to start drinking recklessly. Life's appalling futility goes down a lot better with a good box of wine – it not only protects you from the condescending look of the pedestrians, but it also warms you up and, most important, keeps you company. Actually, wine is such good company that, sooner or later, you realize that you do not need much of anything else to survive. That is the turning point, when you start to forgo everything, so you can bankroll the precious liquid. Wine for breakfast, wine for snacks and wine for sleeping; wine to laugh and wine to cry. Wine at any time possible. And if there is some heroin around, so much the better.

A Season in Hell

I start out with foil smoking, but foil has a foul, metallic aftertaste, so I quickly switch to injection. Trouble is, the more I shoot up, the less visible my blood vessels become, and then it gets messy, so I start scouting for new body parts – virgin areas, if you will – and I test them out. But the problem is the same: I shoot up so much that my veins get blocked, and the process becomes convoluted. So I start asking other people for help to shoot up where I can't reach. The rules for asking another person to shoot you up are straightforward: you share, or you pay. But I cannot afford even the minimum. And that is when I decide to put a price tag on my body. The problem is that the johns seeking sexual service from a junkie are usually other junkies, and they are as penniless as the service provider, but it is what it is, and I do not complain. From Plaza Mayor, I move to an industrial area outside of the city with a group of prostitutes and settle in something resembling a hut.

The Industrial Area

The hut is tiny but has a mattress and a hot plate – to reheat food – and a bathroom with a toilet but no shower. I look hideous, and I realize that there are plenty of girls more attractive than me out there, but I do not care until I notice that I have fewer clients with each passing day, and making ends meet is an uphill battle. One evening, when I could not get even a single coin, a man offered me three euros, and I accepted right away. I know I should not accept anything less than five euros – it is the law of the land – but I am so desperate that I take his money without hesitation. My fellow workers find out, and as soon as I return home, they all beat me up and leave me senseless on the floor. I try to look for another hut, but it is very difficult because word spreads fast, and no whore will take me now. Dawn is fast approaching, and I am drained and freezing to death. I gather pieces of cardboard, get under a bridge and fall asleep.

Zombie

When I wake, I try to stand up, but I cannot. I fall down each time I try to take a step forward. I have difficulty breathing, I ask for help, but after one look, people dash away. My knees buckle; I am dizzy, and my heart is racing. To top it all off, after intense dry heaving, I throw up on myself. I am the walking dead. My body is cramping, and I am about to pass out. I lean on what I think is a wall but soon realize it is a shop window. On the other side of the glass, I see someone who reminds me of myself. At first, I think it is a mere reflection, but soon I realize that it is no reflection: it is a poster of my face. A billboard, with my picture, and below, a little heading that reads: 'In Celebration of the Fifth Centenary of the birth of Santa Teresa. Complete Event Calendar on our website.'

Warranty Certificate

If you google my name, in less than a second, you get over seventy million results – films, paintings, songs, biographies, coffee mugs, exhibits, T-shirts, conferences. I was aware that I had been someone important in life. What I did not know is that after my death, I had become über-famous. My work has been translated into all world languages. And, apart from being a saint, I am: first woman author in modern Spain, a precursor of the Spanish Golden Age, doctor *honoris causa*, language authority, captain of all the Spanish Kingdoms and the pinnacle of experimental mysticism. There's even a dessert named after me. Do you know what they call it? *Yemas*, egg yolks, of Santa Teresa. They are small balls made of egg yolks and covered in confectioners' sugar. Look, here is a box if you fancy a bite. They are all handmade. It says right here: 'Warranty certificate. The authentic and original *Yemas* of Santa Teresa.'

Let's get back on track: I am a pioneer, a groundbreaker, an authority. Not only am I 'an outstanding and exceptional example of the strength and spirit of our culture' but also the 'patron saint of each and every writer in this country'. But what is a patron saint supposed to do? What are the duties? To sponsor and to protect. That's fine. But to sponsor and to protect – how? And, most important, from what or from whom? Where is the enemy?

To Be a Writer in Spain

So I start researching the living situation of authors in Spain, and I soon find out that, 'Nowadays, 85 per cent of Spanish authors scrape to get by, and only 15 per cent can actually make a living writing'. It is important to note that two-thirds of that 15 per cent are men and one-third women, which means that only 5 per cent of women writers make a living out of their profession. And that is not even the worst part. What is truly outrageous is that this tiny percentage is the highest ever for women in the history of this country! Has the quality of life of Spanish women writers evolved at all since I died? The answer is devastating: only 1 per cent every century. And right then, I remember a phrase I had recently read by a writer named Larra: 'To write in Spain is to cry.' To which, years later, another writer with the last name Cernuda would add: 'To write in Spain is not to cry; to write in Spain is to die.' And I think: 'Teresa, every superhero needs an outfit to put on, and you've already got yours on. You only lack a mission, which very well could be this one, which has just been presented to you.' So quick off the mark, I run out of the internet café and go to El Corte Inglés, the department store, and steal a spray can and then to the Congreso de los Diputados, the parliament, the constitutional body that represents all Spaniards. And spray can in hand, I paint on the façade: 'To write in Spain is not to cry, to write in Spain is to die', signed Larra and Cernuda. I immediately climb on the back of one of the lions guarding the entrance to the parliament and start to shout, one by one, the names and surnames of each and every Spanish woman writer, the sadly forgotten authors of this country:

Cristobalina Fernández de Alarcón
Ana Caro
María de Zayas
Juliana Morell
Marcela del Carpio
María Rosa de Gálvez
Gertrudis Gómez de Avellaneda
Carolina Coronado
Concepción Arenal
María Mendoza
Rosario de Acuña
Sofía Casanova
Carmen de Burgos
Concha Espina
María de la O Lejárraga
María de Maeztu
Zenobia Camprubí
Clara Campoamor
Margarita Nelken
Concha Méndez
Rosa Chacel
Ernestina de Champourcín
Josefina de la Torre

Luisa Carnés
Federica Montseny
Carmen Conde
Alfonsa de la Torre
Ángela Figuera
Julia Uceda
María Victoria Atencia

And right at the moment that I shout this last name, María Victoria Atencia, someone grabs me by the back; they shackle me and take me to a nearby police station.

Maximum Penalty

At the police station, I tell everyone the truth, that I am Santa Teresa de Jesús, but no one believes me. They read me my rights and lock me up for the night. The next morning, they take me to a sort of pavilion: a fenced area full of surveillance, where they leave me with other inmates. Inmates, as I soon find out, who are in the same situation I am: women who are drug addicts, undocumented and suffering from some mental disorder. The police accuse me in court, seeking a six-year prison sentence for disorderly conduct, resisting authority and a crime against fundamental rights. The Prosecutor's Office, meanwhile, asks for only nine months in jail and a fine of one thousand eight hundred euros. In my defence, I argue that I did it to restore the dignity of the women writers of Spain. They are exemplary citizens, the true pillars of this country. They empower, dignify and honour Spain. But the cops argue that when the security forces tried to get me off the lion, I showed 'an attitude of contempt towards the officers by kicking and spitting in their faces'. No surprise here: in the end, I get the maximum penalty.

Jail

Life in jail is repetitive and quite boring. If it weren't for the fact that there's a library, where I am all the time, I don't know what would have become of me. The library is almost always closed because, among other reasons, it is understaffed. While the gatekeeper and the cooks have dedicated tasks, the other employees have to cover many jobs and can hardly cope. Eduardo, for example, the warden, takes on janitorial duties; Catalina, one of the cleaners, also organizes gym activities; and Aurora, the head of the infirmary, takes care of the library while running the morgue. She is twice my height, weighs two hundred kilos more than I do and has such a big heart it does not fit in her chest. Every time inmates die, she is the one who puts them in a coffin and buries them in the small cemetery a few kilometres from the compound. Since we are all illegal, we don't have family or official papers, and funerals don't require any kind of mourning or farewells. Aurora places the corpse inside the coffin and, the next day, buries it whenever she wants. She has a daughter sick with leukaemia and hardly a day goes by when she doesn't tell me about her. It comforts her, she says. Aurora is certain that her daughter has very little time left and will soon die. Aurora and I spend so much time together that, one day, by surprise, we discover we have become friends. Such good friends, actually, that, one morning, Aurora decides she is going to leave me the key, so I can enter and leave the library anytime I want.

The Library

At the library, I devour everything from comics to art history books, encyclopedias and DVDs. Is there anything better than cinema? I don't know, but if I could, I would become a film director. Yes, I would love to direct my own films. What would they be about? What if I adapted my writings to film scripts? Can you imagine? *The Interior Castle*, a film by Teresa de Jesús. Would people come to see it? I don't know, but I take so much refuge in film, in the lives of all those characters, that, once again, I forget who I am. Until, one afternoon, when I'm near to exhausting the library's collections, I get into the documentary section and, surprise surprise, I come across a video where I am the subject! Or rather, a documentary where my hand is discussed. Specifically, they discuss this hand right here: my left hand.

The General and I

According to the documentary, someone named General Franco claimed my hand from some nuns in Ronda. Apparently, he needed it because he was convinced it would help him to correctly guide and govern the country. He was so obsessed with my hand that he would take it everywhere he deemed necessary, as if it were a talisman. This means that if the general stayed in El Pardo, my hand stayed in El Pardo; if the general moved to his summer residence, the Pazo de Meirás, my hand came along. And if the general wanted to go salmon fishing, with the salmon expedition I would go. Suffice it to say that the General had a special glass box mounted on his car's glove compartment, so my hand would travel with him wherever he went. As you can see, the General and I were, for a while, practically inseparable until, one day, the General dies, and my hand stays on his bedside table, next to where his corpse rests. They bury the General and take my hand back to the city of Ronda, and there it stays until, as I said at the beginning of our conversation, I jump the walls of La Merced Church. I take it, and I tweak it again to my wrist.

Life's a Joke

Yes, this same hand that, while it was a part of my body, was disavowed by Christianity. However, when it came back to me, I had been made a Doctor of the Church. This same hand that, while it was a part of my body, took a vow of poverty. However, when it came back to me, it did so adorned with jewels and precious stones. This same hand that, while it was a part of my body, was educated in the Jewish faith. However, when it came back to me, I had been made a Saint of the Spanish Race. This same hand that, while it was a part of my body, was fully opposed to marriage. However, when it came back to me, I was made the patron of the Women's Section, a highly conservative take on women's rights that the Dictatorship had created! Is this what I have become? What's the point of writing a book if no one reads it? Life is a joke. And, as soon as I had finished watching that documentary, something came alive within me, yet again. A path, made of shining stones, that led to a door: the jail gate. 'You have to get out of this place and face the world again, Teresa. Do whatever you need to do, but do it. No one has understood a single thing you wrote! No one has understood any of your ideas! That explains why you have become a symbol of everything you stood against. You cannot stay put now; you need to do something right away.' I then remembered one of the first films I watched, shortly after entering jail. I took it and gave it to Aurora to take home and watch.

The Final Escape

The film takes place in a jail where a woman prisoner, like all the other inmates, tries to get used to her lack of freedom. One day, the prisoner meets the second character in this story: a warden, who is also in charge of the infirmary, and he is also in charge of the morgue. Time passes and they become very good friends. One day, the warden reveals that her granddaughter is sick and needs an operation as soon as possible. The woman prisoner then promises that if he helps her escape, once outside, she will give him the money he needs for his granddaughter's operation. 'But how will you escape without anyone discovering what we have done?' the warden asks. 'There's a way,' the inmate replies. 'When the next inmate dies, I will get inside the coffin, and you will bury us both. At night, you will return to the cemetery and get me out. The oxygen stored in the coffin is enough to last me until I'm out again. If you help me, I promise you that once I'm out, I will give you the money to cure your granddaughter's illness.'

A Miracle

As soon as she had seen the film, Aurora told me, 'It's not money my daughter needs, Teresa; my daughter is so sick, she needs a miracle.' Although Aurora trusted me, she never actually believed what I had told her about my life. That all changed a month later, when an inmate died. Aurora had no choice but to accept the complete truth of everything I had been telling her. That day, her daughter, miraculously, was cured; no trace of her disease remained.

A New Path

That's how, the next day, in the middle of a dark night, Aurora dug me up, hugged me tightly, as you do when you realize that you might not see that person ever again, and watched me as I walked out of the cemetery. Once again, I was alone and lost. Again, I had to find my own path. 'The most prudent thing is to start making a living like a normal person. I have to find a job,' I thought. 'But what kind of job?' And it occurred to me that I could stand at a corner of the Rastro, the Sunday flea market, and tell my story to anyone willing to listen. And, hey, people seemed to like me and that helped me to get ahead.

The Monologue

It was tough at the beginning, but, as the weeks passed, I started feeling in control, and, every Sunday, I was collecting at least two hundred euros. More than a monologue, my routine was sort of a variety show, where I would combine episodes of my life with, for example, explanations of my literary works. Look, here are the books. Would you like me to explain them to you? Listen carefully.

Oeuvre

According to scholars, six of my works are key to my Litproduction/ oeuvre. On the one hand, there is my first book, *The Book of Life*, fresh and spontaneous, an honest portrayal of my character and personality. Then there is *The Way of Perfection*, a little more practical and specific, in which I make recommendations for living in the convent. Third, *The Mansions: The Interior Castle*, in which I change my register and move to another phase of my career. Here, I reflect on what it means to become a spiritual being. This is one of my best; I highly recommend it. Then we have *The Book of the Constitutions*, a more juridical and legislative take on the style and customs of the religious order. And to conclude, perhaps the most special, *The Foundations*, clearly my most mature work, in which I mix popular wisdom with events of the time. The truth is that while I am very fond of them all, my poetry is my pride. Yes, without a doubt, of all my work, *The Poems* is what has ended up going viral.

I live without living

I live without living in me,
And such is my hope,
That I die, for I die not.

I now live outside myself
Since I am dying from love;
Because I live in the Lord
Who sought me for Himself.
When I gave Him my heart,
He placed this sign on it:
That I die, for I die not.

This divine prison
Of love with which I live
Has made God my captive
And my heart free,
Causing in me such a pity
To see God my prisoner
That I die, for I die not.

Oh, how long is this life!
How hard these wanderings,
This cell and these irons
In which the soul is held!
Just waiting to get out
Causes me such fierce pain,
That I die, for I die not.

Oh, how bitter the life
That enjoys not the Lord!
For though the love is sweet,
The long wait is not;
May God from me remove this burden
Heavier than steel,
That I die, for I die not.

With only the confidence
That I must die do I live,
For in life's dying
I am assured of my hope.
Death, in which life is found,
Delay not; I await you so
That I die, for I die not.

Behold how love is strong;
Life, be not an annoyance:
See that all you need
To be won is to be lost.
Let now sweet death come;
So do I want airy death to come,
That I die, for I die not.

That life up above,
Which is the true life
Until this life dies,
Is not enjoyed while alive.
Death, avoid me not;
So let me first live, dying
That I die, for I die not.

Life, what can I give you,
To my God, who lives in me,

If it is not to lose you
In order to deserve to win today?
For so much do I love my Beloved,
That I die, for I die not.

Hitting It Big

And, naturally, those who come to hear me freak out. A woman who looks like a junkie says that she is Santa Teresa and recites her poetry. Soon, so many people gather around me it gets too crowded, and I need to find another place. I move to a spot in a square with a fountain. And right there, next to that fountain, I hit it big. I feel it because I see certain faces every day, and what used to be a weekend show only is now daily, with several matinees. Since I do not want my regulars to get bored, in between poems, I decide to insert episodes from my life – a kind of assortment of my vicissitudes from five hundred years ago and from the present. For instance, I compare how five hundred years ago, the nuns wanted me arrested and my arrest at the Parliament. I also establish a dialogue between my first levitations five centuries ago and all the theories claiming that the reason I perceived my feet not touching the ground was simply that I was high as a kite.

LSD

Did you know that, in 1943, Dr Hofmann successfully synthesized lysergic acid from the fungus that grows on rye when it rots? I had no idea. But due to the vow of poverty I took five centuries ago, I ate only the stalest bread in the convent. Some argue now that my levitation was simply the result of consuming the equivalent of many LSD tabs. Do you know what a tab is? A tab is a drop of lysergic acid dissolved on a piece of blotter paper. You place the blotter paper under your tongue until it dissolves like candy. All new to me. While researching this topic, I found a webpage where they sell tabs. The whole piece of blotter paper, divided into twenty-five tabs, will run you one hundred and twenty-five euros. And they all have different names, depending on the printed drawing. The most famous are the Bicycles, the Panoramix, the Aliens, the Acid House, the Buddhas, the Simpsons, the Mickey Mouse, the Superman. Others have my name: Santa Teresa. Have you ever seen them? Look at them – here they are: tabs with my face on them. Look carefully: down here, I'm dealing with many issues, and up here, you see a kind of glow that comes down from the sky in the shape of a dove. Feel free to pass them on, so you can appreciate all the little details. If anyone wants to try one, go ahead. However, I would strongly recommend that first-timers start with just one tiny corner.

Inside Trip

Drugs are not prohibited because they are bad for your health. Drugs are prohibited because, like culture, they are a key that helps you to go farther. A tab and a book are very similar because they prompt a journey. They are vehicles that transport you from this world to a different one that others cannot see, but it is there. Drugs are prohibited because they push you to the limit; they enlighten you; and while you are on that threshold, they reveal the truth to you. That is why the powers-that-be constantly criminalize drugs, and also culture, simply because they manage to open the doors of the brains of those who consume them, and they can clearly reveal all kinds of falsehood and hypocrisy. In 1969, during the three days of the Woodstock festival, three million people lived together under the effects of lysergic acid. Not a single case of suicide or assault caused by the substance was reported. At the same time, outside the festival, thousands of sober people were committing murder or suicide or rape. If instead of working so hard, human beings read and did more drugs, politicians would quickly vanish into thin air. Because knowledge is indeed a weapon of mass destruction, and the first thing it does is blow the idea of power right away. That is why we are only allowed to consume drugs that anchor us to this world and never those that lead us to another reality. Yes, travel is strictly prohibited. We believe that we move because our body can move through space, but the reality is that from the moment we are born until we die, few of us manage to move from where we are. And contrary to what they want us to believe, true movement is not physical; true movement is achieved through the mind and has a name: inner trip.

An Unexpected Twist

One afternoon, at about this point in the monologue, a young woman comes up to me and hands me a card and says, 'I own a theatre café, sort of a comedy club, where people try out their stand-up comedy routines'. 'Stand-up comedy? What is that'? I ask. 'Could you do the same thing you do right here on the street on stage'? she asks. Oh well. In less than a week, not only had I met with her, I was at her theatre café, blabbing my monologue. This time, I add a political debate to my reflections. It's a round table in which I interact with the audience, examining such questions as: Why are Spaniards the way we are? In what areas have we advanced as a society in the last five hundred years, and in what others have we not? And a very important question: To what extent do you think the four centuries that the Holy Inquisition has ruled our country have manipulated our character? For whatever reason, the monologue is successful, a lot of people come to see me, and Virginia, the owner of the theatre, decides to include me as a regular. The truth is that Virginia makes me feel wonderful. First, because I have found a true friend and, second, because with the money I earn, I can finally afford a room in a hostel and, for the first time, I have my own home.

God's Ways Are Inscrutable

The room is small, and there's no view of the street. My windows overlook an inside patio, but I like it because I do not get distracted and can concentrate more. In the morning, I polish my monologue, then I eat something, anything, followed by a nap, and when I awake, I go into the bathroom and begin to deconstruct myself. I sit on the edge of the tub and, limb by limb, I take myself apart. First a foot, then a nose, then I take off my eyes, my intestines, my bones, my eyelashes – then, floating in the tub, I can finally rest, free from the weight of the flesh.

And, as I attentively watch all my limbs floating in the water, I ask myself, 'What if everyone else is right, and I'm the wrong? What if, just like everyone says, I am just a demented woman and not a true saint? Am I fully convinced of who I am?' At a quarter to seven, the alarm goes off. I start gathering all my limbs while still in the tub, and I put myself back together bit by bit. I look in the mirror before leaving my room and heading out once again towards the cafeteria. I look at myself and think, 'I came back to life for a second time without knowing who I was or what purpose Heaven had for me, and now, look at me: I'm not a nun or a slut; neither a delinquent nor a beggar nor a junkie nor a convict: I'm an actress and a DJ.' I'm an actress because that's how I make a living, and I'm a DJ because, ever since Virginia took me out to a house party in an abandoned building, my life took a one-hundred-and-eighty degree turn. And just as I had about five hundred years ago, I have another revelation, but this time I'm in the middle of a dance floor, surrounded by thousands of women dancing to techno music.

Second Revelation

A space dedicated to experimental music where all goods are shared and social status is irrelevant; a home where everyone's individuality is respected, and riches are despised. A humble living space dedicated to techno music. It's neither a convent nor a dance hall. Ecstasy, trance and sweat: a home for expansion and the contemplative life. Not just a temple but a beacon that shines light upon the rest of the world. Yes, Teresa, you must walk towards the edge of the precipice. You must stop at the edge of the cliff, and then you must jump. Jump without any fear, for fear is the devil, and your only obligation is to go deeper into the unknown. You shall carry it out even though you may feel threatened, and they will deem you a danger. And in that precise moment – in that moment, as you did five hundred years ago, you will change your name once again. You will no longer be Teresa de Jesús, but this time, you will use your initials, and you will be known as Teresa DJ. A woman with a mission: to occupy as many houses as possible, so you can officiate your ceremonies; you will perform rites that will let the world stop being an end and start being a means. A gate through which the soul of all the people gathered may gain strength and, filled with God's love, take flight.

Floating in Ecstasy

This is exactly what I did: I recovered the same spaces I had conquered five hundred years ago, so I can play electronic music inside the convents.

A DJ booth descends from the roof. The woman puts on headphones, turns on the DJ booth and begins to play progressive trance music. Stroboscopic lights flash everywhere.

From Avila to Medina del Campo, from Medina del Campo to Malagon, from Malagon to Valladolid, from Valladolid to Toledo, from Toledo to Pastrana, from Pastrana to Salamanca, from Salamanca to Alba de Tormes, from Alba de Tormes to Segovia, and from Segovia to Beas de Segura. When suddenly, while I'm in the booth, something paranormal happens to me yet again. These seemingly otherworldly psychedelic lights suddenly fill the room and welcome a cherub, a luminous angel that, in mid-air, aims a golden arrow at my chest. An incandescent arrow that, after striking me to the ground, makes something rise from my throat. It is my heart, turned into a dove, flying out of my mouth, flying over everyone, a dove as white as snow, followed by a flame that burns everything in its path. Once everything is up in flames, the dove flies close to me and says,

'Teresa, what does it matter if you were a saint who never stopped seeking God or just a woman seeking only herself? What does it matter if, in the end, everything you said and did aimed to protect the dignity of others – their dignity and especially God's dignity, which is just your need to roam free, your desire for knowledge and your hunger for freedom? Freedom to be both hermit and wanderer, contemplative mystic and garrulous woman, enlightened soul and cynical impostor.' And as it was speaking these last words, the dove plummeted by my side. A dead dove now lay on the ground, then suddenly transformed into a puddle of dark water, a pit as dark as night. When I tried to look over it, I fell in. 'What if in order to discover *who I truly am*,' I thought as my body fell swiftly through the black hole, 'I had to escape from everything I thought I was? What if in order to discover *who I truly am*, I had to escape from my personality's set ways? And what if in order to discover *who we truly are*, we have to escape as far away as possible until we completely lose ourselves and finally disappear?'

The woman removes her headphones, gets down from the stage and begins to dance among the crowd with an inextinguishable joy. The following message appears projected over the front wall of the auditorium:

Those who wish to achieve everything must renounce everything.

Teresa Sánchez de Cepeda Dávila y Ahumada

At that moment, the theatre is no longer a theatre – it's a sanctuary, a temple, tenebrous, yet filled with light. The audience is standing up, dancing as if there were no past or future, only the present. A continuous present, endless, that connects them to eternity